NEW YORK
HISTORICAL MANUSCRIPTS

MINUTES OF THE MAYORS COURT OF NEW YORK, 1674-1675

NEW YORK
HISTORICAL MANUSCRIPTS

MINUTES OF THE
MAYORS COURT OF NEW YORK,
1674-1675

Edited by
KENNETH SCOTT

Published under the Direction of
The Holland Society of New York

Baltimore
GENEALOGICAL PUBLISHING CO., INC.

To the memory of

LOUIS BEACH VREELAND

Past President and Trustee of The Holland
Society of New York whose great interest in
the Dutch families of New Netherland and
their descendants was manifested in his
devotion to and generous support
of the Society.

PREFACE

The discovery by Kenneth Scott of the long lost New York Mayors Court records for 1674-75 is a significant event in documentary history, filling a gap in our knowledge of a critical period. Since Albany's court records for this period were also lost (and still are), we have until now had only Kingston's records for local reaction to the final English takeover of New York, and in fact Kingston was little affected.

We find a different situation in New York City. Among the members of the new court were two members of the Governor's Council, and many of the litigants were government officials. As the seat of government and the site of the colony's chief port, New York would produce many court suits of significance beyond the city limits.

The relationship between the local court and the provincial government during the first formative year of the Andros administration has previously been known only from the provincial records, and our knowledge from that source was sharply reduced by the State Capitol fire of 1911. Forty-four of the first eighty-eight pages in Andros' first book of general entries were destroyed, so that in fact we are at a loss as to the number of his orders, letters, instructions, and proclamations to the New York court.

In fact, I was in the process of editing the books of general entries when Dr. Scott made his discovery of the Mayors Court records. He most graciously agreed to let me have a photocopy, which enabled me to resolve several problems of text and chronology in the provincial records.

The publication of this volume of Mayors Court records fills the gap between the two previously published series of Dutch and English records. During the long court adjournment from the end of this book (Sept. 21) to the beginning of the next (Oct. 17), the court attended the colony's General Court of Assizes, with Mayor Nicolls serving as secretary of the court.

The records contain any number of important new insights and will be plumbed enthusiastically by historians. Several cases suggest the disruptions caused by two changes of government in seventeen months. Landlords were suing for two years' back rent. Englishmen returning from exile sued for the return of property ransacked from their homes (and the Governor sued for recovery of a stove taken from the fort!). The urge to fix blame for the earlier surrender to the Dutch led to much fingerpointing such as in the suit between Alderman John Lawrence and Captain John Manning. One important decision attempted to establish the legal ownership of vessels that were seized as prizes of war and sold at auction.

Whether by accident or design the court is representative of the major ethnic groups in the city and, most intentionally, of the better class of citizen. Mayor Nicolls is a career government official; the aldermen are wealthy

New York City merchants. All are self-made men, except possibly Alderman Dervall (his career took off after his marriage to Thomas Delavall's daughter). Despite the Governor's prejudices against New Englanders and the Dutch, both are represented on the court, along with the Royalist mayor and a refugee Frenchman.

In addition to their value as legal and social history, these records contain a considerable amount of biographical data. We note, for example, two references to Joseph Yates in April 1675, the earliest references we have seen to him (more than a year before he appears in the Albany records). Expanding upon the information in the records, Dr. Scott has noted for most individuals additional data from other sources, giving vital statistics, occupations, and alternate forms of names.

Researchers are twice blessed, first that the records were discovered at all, and second that it was Kenneth Scott who discovered them. Dr. Scott's dedication to the disseminating of historical information is evidenced by his production of some forty published volumes. His care in preparing accurate transcripts can be attested to by the curators of the manuscripts he had copied: his attention to detail in transcribing the New York marriage bonds is still mentioned by New York State Library staff a decade later.

Peter Christoph
Associate Librarian,
Manuscripts and Special
    Collections
The New York State Library

INTRODUCTION

A manuscript volume, hitherto unpublished, of the minutes of the Mayors Court of New York, 13 November 1674 – 21 September 1675, in the custody of the County Clerk of New York, is of no little importance for the history of the city and province during the time of Governor Colve and the period immediately after the province came again into the hands of the English.

Numerous cases are concerned with suits arising from attempts by former owners to recover possessions confiscated by the Dutch. The usefulness of these early minutes is enhanced by the fact that records for the time of Governor Andros were partially destroyed in the fire in Albany in 1911 and, further, by the fact that the published Minutes of the Common Council of the City of New York begin on 17 October 1675.

To the transcription of the Mayors Court minutes have been added numerous footnotes in the hope that they will be of value for historical and genealogical research. The notes are based on a limited number of reference works, as is indicated by the list of the works and abbreviations employed, given at the bottom of page 61.

The editor of this volume is indebted for help and encouragement to Norman Goodman, County Clerk and Clerk of the Supreme Court, New York County; to Timothy Patrick Sullivan, First Deputy County Clerk; and to Joseph Van Nostrand of their staff; to The Holland Society of New York; and to Peter Christoph, Associate Librarian, The New York State Library. Mrs. Margo Higgins has given invaluable assistance in the preparation of this book.

Kenneth Scott

NEW YORK
HISTORICAL MANUSCRIPTS

MINUTES OF THE MAYORS COURT OF NEW YORK, 1674-1675

At a Mayors Court held in New Yorke, the 13th of
November, in the 26th yeare of his Majesties Reigne
Annoque Domini 1674.
Present: Capt. Mathias Nicolls, Mayor; Mr. John
Lawrence, Deputy Mayor; Mr. Wm. Darvall, Mr. Fred.
Phillipps, Mr. Gabr. Minviele, Aldermen; Mr. Thom.
Gibbs, Sherriffe.
This day the Worshippfull Court having nominated
John Sharpe of this Citty to bee Towne Clearke, by and
with the approbation of his honor Collonell Edmond An-
dros, the Governour, hee was sworne accordingly.
William White[1] Sworne Constable.
Barnard Jacobs, Francis Leigh, George Cobbett,[2] Wal-
ter Hiatt, William Welch,[3] Claus Dittloo,[4] Richd. Hay-
mor, Jacob Barnson, Geo. Walsgrave,[5] Rogr. Purchase,[6]
Sworne Wine & Corne Porters.
John Watkins,[7] Thom. Griffin,[8] Sym. Lucas,[9] John
Minas, Peter Wessell,[10] Abram. Waram, Willm. Cooke,[11]
Jon. the Pape,[12] Gysbert the Bore, Jon. Kyckout, Claus
Tuynier, Jon. Longstraet,[13] Carmen.
Thomas Moore,[14] City Cryer.
The Court adjourned.

At a Mayors Court held in New Yorke the 17th day of
November, in the 26th yeare of his Majesties Reigne
Annoque 1674.
Present: Mr. Mathias Nicolls, Mayor; Mr. John Law-
rence, Deputy; Mr. Wm. Darvall,[15] Mr. Gab. Minviele,
Mr. Fre. Phillipps, Aldermen.
William Darvall, Plt.
Peter Aldrix, Deft.
John Tudor[16] Attorney for the Plt. declared that
the deft. deteyned a certaine sloope with her ap-
purtenences, belonging to the plt., and desyred
it might be restroed to him againe, alleaging the
Dutch Admiralls had engaged noe Cittysons should
Loose any of their goods, and produced a Coppy of
the same in Dutch, which was read, as alsoe a
Certeficate under 6 Burgers hands, that testified
at the tyme of taking the fort hee, the plt., was
a Burger, and his servants were in his house, in
which hee maintained Fyer and Light, although hee
was personally at Boston. The deft. produced a
bill of sale under the hand of Governor Colve,
for his said Boate, and a Coppy of the Instrument
of Confiscation; after the Court had heard what
both partyes could aleadge, the president gave
the Charge to the Jury who were these following:

Capt. Nath. Davenport,[17] Thomas Wandall, Rodger
Rugg,[18] John Tucker,[19] Henry Perrin, John West,[20]
Dirrick van Cleafe,[21] Wm. Bogardus,[22] Jacob Lockerman,[23] Peter De La Noy,[24] Humph. Davenport,[25] C
Silv. Salisbury,[26] Jurors.
    Whoe brought in their Verdict, That they found
for the Plt., the Restoration of the Boate in Controversye, with her appurtenances and Costs of
Court. The Worshippfull Court Orderd Judgment to
bee entred accordingly, adjudging the said Sloope
or Boate to belong to Mr. Darvall the Plt.

Allard Anthony,[27] Plt.
Thomas Grizell, Deft.
    The Plt. declares the deft. is indebted to him in
    the summe of f. 182.10 & hath attached f. 100 in
    the hands of Derrick Janson.[28] The deft. not ap-
    pearing, the Court ordered that if he appeare not
    the next Court day to shew reasons to the contrary
    Judgment shall then pass against him.

Capt. Mathias Nicolls,[29] Plt.
Greetye Provost,[30] Deft.
    The plt. declared that the deft. had hyred unto
    him some certaine buildings and priviledges ad-
    joyning to his house, and after his exyle, then
    the deft. removed all the said buildings, and
    tooke posession of the premisses converting the
    Same to her owne use and proffit, Notwithstanding
    hee paid the rent for the same, which Buildings
    and conveniences had cost him neare a Thousand
    Guilders, wherefore hee prays the Court to Order
    him the present posession of the premisses, with
    such repayration as was on the Same when the deft.
    tooke it away. The Worshippfull Court haveing ma-
    turely debated on the matter, Ordered that the
    deft. forthwith deliver and make good the same
    within 14 dayes, and the plt. to pay the Deft. her
    rent due for the tyme hee hath enjoyed it, deft.
    to pay Costs.

Thomas Wandall,[31] Plt.
Hugo Barnson,[32] Deft.
    The Plt. declared that the deft. had lived 14
    mondts in his house without paying him his due
    rent or satisfaction for the same, and without his
    consent or lawfull agreement would continue therir
    for the tearme of 3 yeares, wherefore prayed the
    Court to Order the deft. imediatly to depart out
    of his said house, and pay him the rent due. The
    Worshippfull Court having heard what both parties
    could aleage, and examined the wittnesses on both
    sides, Ordered that the deft. make imediate paymer
    of the rent due to the plt. to say after the rate

of 325 Guilders per annum, and put in security to
depart the said house by the first day of May next,
without doeing any dammage to the Same, as alsoe
to pay the rent that then shall bee due, and that
the plt. shall have liberty in the meane tyme, to
build or repayre what hee hath occasion for in or
about the said house, the deft. to pay costs.

Peter Aldrix, Plt.
Wm. Darvall, Deft.
The Plt. declared hee was mistaken in his plea, it
being comprehended in the former acction, whereupon the Worshippfull Court Ordered a Nonsuite
against the plt., and hee to pay the Costs there-
off.

Mr. John Lawrence,[33] Plt.
Capt. John Manning,[34] Deft.
The plt. declared that the deft. had greatly de-
famed and aspersed him, having spread abroad and
told divers persons that hee the plt., might have
Savid the Mace & Gownes if hee would, but hee delivered them to the Dutch without order. The plt.
proved that hee was forced therunto and produced
the Dutch Governor's Order for his delivering the
Same. The deft. not appearing, the Court Judged
the said reports of the deft. were untrue and un-
deserving.

Robert Hollis,[35] Plt.
Tho. Hatfeild,[36] Deft.
The deft. appeared but the Plt. was absent, wherefore the Court Ordered a nonsuite against the plt.,
with Costs.

Order: The Court finding great inconveniencies attend-
ing them by the bringing in writings and papers written in the Dutch language doe therefore Order that
for the future noe papers shall be brought to this
Court in Dutch, on the penalty of having them throwne
out, Excepting poore people who are not able to pay
for translating.

Henry Vandyke,[37] Plt.
Allard Anthony, Deft. First Default.

At an Extra Court held the 30th November 1674.
Present: His honnor the Governor; Capt. Griffith;
Capt. Burton; Mr. Mayor & Deputy; Mr. Wm. Darvall, Mr.
fred. Phillips, Mr. Gab. Minviele, Mr. John Winder,
Aldermen.
Proclamation: The Proclamation prohibitting the Ex-
portation of Wheate was this day Published at the Town-
hall.

Mr. Christopher Hoghland[38] being nominated for Surveyor of bread and flower and Gauger, and Richard Elliot[39] for packer, are appoynted to attend the Court next Court day in order to Settling those imployes.

At a Mayors Court held in New Yorke the 1st December in the 26 yeare of his Majesties Reigne Annoque Domini 1674.

Present: Mr. Mathias Nicolls, Mayor; Mr. John Lawrence, Deputy; Mr. William Darvall, Mr. Fred. Phillips, Mr. Gabriel Minviele, Mr. John Winder, Aldermen.

Capt. John Manning this day appeared before Court Satt and acknowledged what hee had reported relating to Mr. John Lawrences his Loosing the Mace and Gownes. It was by misinformation and is very sorry for it, whereupon the Worshippfull Court ordered Capt. Mannings said accknowledgement should bee Recorded to the end the Callumnie Cast on the said Mr. John Lawrence by the said Aspersion may bee taken off.

Mr. Allexander Bryan,[40] Plt.
Elizabeth Bedloo,[41] Deft.

> The Plt. by his Attorney Capt. Nathaniell Davenport attached the house of the deft. for the Summe of £ 129:09:06, the deft. not having as yet Stated her accounts, her sonn appearing for her moved the Court for 3 moneths tyme, which by consent of the plt's Attorney was condesended to, but the Attachment is to remayne and continue on the said house untill a decision is made of the Matter.

Order: The Court being informed that it is a common practice of the Carmen to ryde wood and other things on the Sabeth day, which hath bine formerly forbidden on great penaltyes, as alsoe digging Sand in unlawfull places, to the Great detriment of many, wherefore its Now againe ordered that none presume to doe it, On such penalties as the worshippfull Court shall thinke meet to inflict upon the offenders.

Walter Webly,[42] Plt., Trustee to the estate of Capt. Morris.
Peter Aldrix, Deft.

> The Plt. by his Attorney John Tudor declared that the Deft. deteyned a Negro woman etc. and produced an order of Governor Colves to returne all the goods & Chattells belonging to the Orphane Child and an Order of Collonell Morris to manifest the Negro in controversye, propperly the said Orphans, without any devision or Exception, and the plt. made Oath it was the very same Negro. George Cooke[43] Attorney for the Deft. read his answer to the plts declaracon, alleaging the said Negro was prize and lawfully sold to the deft. being one of

the 18 divided. The Mayor gave the Jury their
Charge who were: Capt. Silvester Salisbury, Mr.
Roger Rugg, Mr. Peter Jacobs,[44] Mr. Wm. White,[45]
Tho. Taylor,[46] Claus Burding,[47] Antho. Waters,[48]
Samuell Blagg,[49] Wm. Merritt,[50] Mat. De Haert,[51]
Hen. Baker,[52] Senior, Dan. De Haert,[53] And brought
in their verdict for the Plt., with Costs. The
Court finding the Negro properly to belong to the
Orphane passed their Judgment accordingly, and
the Deft. to pay Costs of Suite.

Walter Webly, trustee etc., Plt.
Capt. Martine Cregier,[54] Deft.
    At the motion of the Deft. it was suspended untill
    the next Court day to the end the deft. might take
    out a Coppy of the plaintif's Declaration.

John Henry,[55] Plt.
John Smedes,[56] Deft.
    The worshippfull Court finding the matter intri-
    gate Ordered the parties to nominate Arbittrators
    and bring in there names next Court day.

Thomas Lovlace,[57] Plt.
Samuell Rescoe,[58] Deft.
    The Court Ordered the Deft. tyme till next Court
    day to take out a Coppy of the Declaracion.

Capt. John Manning, Plt.
Dirick van Cleyfe, Deft.
    The Court ordered the deft. tyme till next Court
    day to take out a Coppy of the Plaintif's declara-
    cion.

John Sharpe,[59] Plt.
Otto Gerritson,[60] Deft.
    The Plt. declared that the deft. was Indebted un-
    to him per account f. 123.14½; the deft. owned
    the debt. The Worshippfull Court gave Judgment
    that the deft. pay the said summe in 14 dayes in
    the species according to Condition, with Costs.

Mathias Nicolls, Plt.
Greetie Provost, Deft.
    The Plt. complaines that the deft. is remiss in
    not fullfilling the order of the Last Court upon
    which the Worshippfull Court doe Order that the
    plt. to take the premisses into his possession and
    sett upp and repayre the same at the Defendant's
    Charge, and shee to pay Costs.

John Sharpe, Plt.
Thomas Taylor, Deft.
    The plt. declared that the deft. was indebted unto

him in the summe of f. 141.1 and 3/4;   the defendant owned the debt;   the worshippfull Court Ordered Judgment to bee entred against the deft. to
pay the said summe in 14 dayes, with Costs.

Annatye Cregiers, Plt.
John Smedes, Deft.
    The Plt. declared that the deft. was indebted to
    her Tenn Beavers and had a Judgment for the same
    formerly;   the Court ordered that if the deft. did
    not pay it in 8 dayes, then Execution to issue,
    which is since accordingly issued.

Gabriell Minviele,[61] Complainant
John Hendry,[62] Deft.
    The Complainant declares the deft. deteyneth 18
    Cornesacks of his marked ML;   the Worshippfull
    Court Orders the Deft. forthwith to deliver the
    said sacks and Costs.

Fredericke Phillipps,[63] Complainant
Jaques Coussou,[64] Deft.
    The Complainant declares hee hath Judgment and
    execution against the deft. since November 1672
    for the summe of f. 1200 hallan mony with the
    interest at 6 percent and cannot as yet get the
    said Execution Executed.   The Worshippfull Court
    Orders the deft. to appeare the next Court day to
    shew reasons why the said Execution shall not be
    executed. - Otherwise it shall proceed accordingly.

Order for the Corne Porters: Upon the Peticion of the
    Corne Porters & wyne Porters, Shewing their agrei-
    vance by Brewers Bakers and others, setting day
    Laborers on Worke to carry up their corne and other
    things, which of right apperteynes to them.   The
    Court thereupon Orders that the Brewers shall have
    the wyne porters to carry out their Beere as formerly
    was accustomed, and the Bakers are not to hyer or
    permitt any corne to bee Carryed upp or brought downe
    in their houses or Garretts by any other persons then
    their owne Servants, or the Corne Porters.

At a Mayors Court held in New Yorke the 22th December
1674.
    Present: Mr. Mathias Nicolls, Mayor;   Mr. John Law-
rence, Deputy;   Mr. Wm. Darvall, Mr. Fred. Phillipps,
Mr. Gab. Minviele, Mr. John Winder, Aldermen.
    Walter Webley, Plt.
    Martine Cregier, Deft.
        The deft. not appearing, the worshippfull Court
        ordered that Judgment bee entred against him for
        the whole summe of f. 576 if the deft. does not by
        the next Court day shew reason to the Contrary,

the deft. to pay costs.

Fredrick Phillipps, Plt.
Jaques Cousou, Deft.
    The Plt. moves for Execution to bee Executed
against the deft.; the defendant's Attorney moved
for tyme to sell the estate to make him payment;
the Court requested the plt. to consider of it
against the next Court day.

Thomas Lovlace, Plt.
Samuell Rescoe, Deft.
    The Plt. declares for £ 10:16:00 due upon account;
the deft. moved for a Coppy of the account and
declaracion against next Court; the Worshippfull
Court did order it accordingly.

Capt. John Manning, Plt.
Dirrick van Cleyfe, Deft.
    The Plt. declared in an accion of trespass on the
Case for deteyning a certaine house and ground
hee bought of one Martine Hoffman[65] and hath had
the peaceable posession thereof neare 5 yeare and
prayes the said house and premisses may be imed-
iatly restored to him, with the rents and proff-
itts thereof; the Court advizes both parties to
a Composure by the next Court day, otherwise then
a Jury shall bee impanelled to goe theron.

Thomas Taylor, Plt.
Fredrick the Cooper,[66] Deft.
    The deft. not appearing, the worshippfull Court
Orders Judgment to bee entred against him but noe
execution to bee issued till next Court.

Henry Van Dyke, Plt.
Allard Anthony, Deft.
    The plt. declared that by the Insufficiency of the
defendant's fence hee was greatly damnified, Cattell and hoggs having therby destroyed his Orchard
and fruite trees, the defendant alleaging the winter was soe hard that hee could not repayre the
same untill the weather broke up; the Worshippfull Court Ordered the deft. to doe it with all
possible speede hee Could.

Olave Steephens,[67] Plt.
Capt. John Manning, Deft.
    The plt. bringing in his declaracion, the Court
ordered the deft. to take out a Coppie against the
next Court day.

John Henry, Plt.
John Smedes, Deft.
   The plt. declares the deft. will not perform the
   award of the Arbitrators and hath broken his bond,
   Wherefore the Court thought fitt to order Judgment for the deft. to fullfill the award of the
   said arbitrators and to pay Costs but noe Execution until next Court day or Further order.

Thomas Gibbs,[68] Sherriff, Plt.
Otto Gerritson, Deft.
   The Plt. declared that the Deft. contrary to Law
   Sold drinke without a Lycence. The deft. answered Mr. Clearke and Mr. Davenport, the Collectors
   for the Tappers Excize, ordered and impowred him
   soe to doe; the Court orders that the deft. make
   it appeare against the next Court day.

Ditto, Sherriff, Plt.
Sigismundus Carman,[69] Deft.
   The Plt. declared hee commanded the deft. by the
   Governor's order to Cart downe a Caske but hee
   refused the doeing thereof. Wm. White the Constable testified that hee with the Staff Commanded the Like but the deft. replyed hee would not
   Cart for the Governor nor nobody else, wherefore
   the Court Ordered that hee shall Cart noe more
   untill the Court thinkes meete to admitt him therunto.

Paulus Vander Beake,[70] Plt.
Hans De Norman, Deft.
   The Plt. declares the deft. bought of him a Certaine quantity of Apples, for which hee is indebted f. 92:01 and prayes Judgment with Costs. The
   Worshippfull Court Orders Judgment to bee entred
   and that the deft. pay 2/3 and the plt. 1/3 of
   the Costs.

Thomas Gibbs, Sherriff, Plt.
Arient Isackson [71] & wife, Defendants.
   The plt. declares the defendants frequently breake
   the peace of our Soveraigne lord the King by fighting and beating each other. This being the defendants' 2d default, the Court orders that they
   appeare next Court day on the penalty of one
   hundred guilders, and if they committ any enormi-
   ty in the meane tyme, the sherriff is to Committ
   the offenders to prison.

Alice Manning,[72] Plt.
Katherne Harrison,[73] Deft.
   The defendant's first default.

Mr. Gabriell Minviele, Plt.
Claus Lock,[74] Deft.
    The Plt. declared that the deft. owed him on bal-
lance of accounts f. 227.10 in Wampom and prays
Judgment with Costs. The Court advized both partyes to compose it if possible by Arbitrators,
otherwise to have it determined the next Court day.

Sherriff Gibbs, Plt.
Dirrick Van Cleyfe, Deft.
    The Plt. declared hee had, by the Governor's
order, attached the house wherin the deft. now
lived next adjoyning to the Citty Hall, formerly
belonging to Coll. Francis Lovelace, for the account of his Royall highness. The deft. answered
hee had hyred it from Nicolas Bayard[75] and produced his Lease to prove the same. The deft. own-
ing hee had as yet paid noe rent, the Worshippfull
Court orderd him to pay noe rent for the said
house untill hee had Order from his honnor the
Governor or this Court.

Sherriff Gibbs, Plt.
        Pardon,[76] Deft.
    The Plt. declared hee had by the Governor's Order
attached the house in the broad way in which the
deft. now Lived, formerly belonging to Collonnell
Lovelace, on his Royall highnesses account. The
deft. informed the Court hee was put in it by the
order of Capt. Phillip Carterett.[77] The Worshippfull Court alsoe ordered him to pay noe rent till
further Order.

Sherriff Gibbs, Plt.
Dirrick Seekers,[78] Deft.
    The Plt. declared the deft. was a tennant on the
farme or the 2 pecces of Land Lying without the
land gate which formerly belonged to
The deft. informed the Court hee had paid f. 207
hallands money rent for the same. The Court ordered him to pay noe more untill further order.

Jaculyne Turneur,[79] Plt.
Elizab. Nachtingale,[80] Deft.
    The Plt. declared that the deft. had greatly de-
famed her husband deceased, etc.. The Court ordered that it being formerly determined, the deft.
shall either at harlam or in this Court make her
Accknowledgment and pay all Costs.

Nathaniell Brittaine,[81] Plt.
Wm. Osborne[82] & Fran. Dowty,[83] Defendants
    John Sharpe[84] Attorney for the plt., declared that
    the defendants were Bayle in anno 16 for Mr.
    Francis Doughty who was arrested and in the Prison
    of this Citty where Judgment passed against the
    said Francis for 1900 lbs. of Tobacoe, with Costs.
    The said Francis having absented himselfe allmost
    ever since and hath not performed the said Judg-
    ment, the plt. is forced to crave Justice against
    the Defendants that Execution may bee granted
    against them to fullfill the said Judgment with
    Costs and interest, The Worshippfull Court Order-
    ed that if the Defendants having notice hereof
    doe not Shew reason to the Contrary next Court day
    Execution shall bee issued forth against them
    accordingly.

John Sharpe, Plt.
John Rider,[85] Deft.
    The Plt. declared that he had obteyned a Judgment
    against John Rider and William Cruchlow[86] for the
    summe of f. 483.10 with Costs from the Mayors
    Court holden June 3, 1673 and Craves Execution
    thereupon. The Worshippfull Court ordered that if
    the Deft. did not shew reasons to the contrary
    next Court day, Execution should bee Exhibited
    accordingly.

At a Mayors Court held in New Yorke the 19th January
1674/5.
    Present: Capt. Math. Nicolls, Mayor; Mr. John Law-
rence, Deputy; Mr. Fre. Phillipps, Mr. Gab. Minviele,
Mr. John Winder, Aldermen.
    Thomas Lovelace, Plt.
    Samuell Rescoe, Deft.
        The plt. and deft. appearing, the Worshippfull
        Court advized them to put their difference to
        arbitracion and if they Could not agree, then to
        determine it next Court.

Walter Webley, Plt.
Martine Cregier, Deft.
        The Plt. by his attorney, Mr. Cooke, Declared that
        hee delivered unto the Deft. certaine goods in
        trust ammounting to the value of f. 576 but sundry
        of them are wanting, and prayes Satisfaction. The
        defendant replyes that they were taken away from
        him by virtue of an order from Governor Colve, as
        hee produced in Court, which was only under the
        hand of Nicolas Bayard. The Worshippfull Court
        ordered Judgment to bee entred against the Defen-
        dant to make good the promisses to the plt. and
        pay Costs, and if the deft. see cause, hee hath

his remedye at Law against the said Nicolas Bayard.

Capt. John Manning, Plt.
Derrick Van Cleyffe, Deft.
 The plt. declared that the deft. detyned a Certaine house and appurtenances from him, lying in
the Broadway in this Citty, which hee had bought,
paid for and had had the quiet posession thereof
about 5 yeares, without the Lest claime or hin-
derance of the deft., and produced the Pattent
and Bill of Sale for the same. The deft. alleadged the said house was mortgaged to One
Moosman[87] before the said Sale, which said Moosman imployed the deft. to bee his Attorney but is
since deceased, whereupon the Plaintif's Attorney
pleaded the defendant's power deyd - Actio Mor-
ritter cum Persona. A Jury being impanalled, the
president gave them their charge. Jurors: Mr.
Edward Dyer, [88] Mr. Hum. Davenport, Mr. Sam. Edsall,[89] Mr. Josep. Knott,[90] John Shackerly,[91]
Tho. Lewis, Nat. Spratt, Anto. De Milt, Claus
Burding, Peter Jacobs, Corn. V. Bursen, Luyc. Ten-
enhoven,[93] who went out and brought in their verdict as follows: Theyre verdict being Speciall,
they find the Mortgage to bee good but the plaintif to have posession of the house and each to
beare his owne charges as to Costs of suite and
the Juryes charge to bee divided betweene them.
The Worshippfull Court order Judgment to be entred
accordingly.

Capt. William Dyre,[94] for his R. Highness, Plaintiff.
Mr. Egidius Luke,[95] Defendant.
 By Consent, this Case is Ordered to bee heard Next
Court day.

Thomas Taylor, Plaintiff
Fred. the Cooper,[96] Defendant.
 The Plaintiff declares the Defendant is indebted
unto him in the summe of f.   . The Defendant having made 2 defaults, the Worshippfull
Court Order Judgment to be entred against the defendant, with Costs.

Henry Vandyke, Plaintiff.
Allard Anthony, Defendant.
 The Plaintiff declares, by the neglect of the defendant in keeping his fence in good repayre, hee
is greatly damnified in his Garden & the trees in
his orchard destroyed by coming in of Cattell,
hoggs, etc. The Worshippfull Court, having heard
what both parties doe alleage, doe Order that the
defendant doe make good and repayre his part of

the fence, and for the damage there shall bee persons appoynted to view the same and bring in their report to the Court.

Olave Steevens, Plaintiff
Capt John Manning, Defendant.
   The Defendant is ordered to take out a Coppy of the plaintiff's Declaration against the next Court day.

Paulus Vander Beake, Plaintiff
Hans the Norman, Defendant.
   The worshippfull Court doe Order the former Judgment to bee Executed.

Alice Manning, Plaintiff
Kath. Harrison, Defendant.
   This being the 2d default in the defendant, the Worshippfull Court doe Order that if the Defendant doe not appeare next Court day then Judgment Shall bee entred against her.

Gabriell Minviele, Plaintiff
Claus Lock, Defendant.
   The Court order to suspend it till next Court.

Cornellis Corsen,[97] Plaintiff
Arian Cornelison,[98] Defendant.
   The Plaintiff not appearing, the Court orders if hee doe not presente his accion next Court day a Nonsuite shall bee the Issue.

George Downing,[99] Plaintiff
Allert Bush,[100] Defendant.
   The Plaintiff by his Attorney Mr. Cooke declares that the defendant deteyneth a Gunn of his and 12 Guilders in wampom. Both parties being heard, the Worshippfull Court order Judgment to be entred against the defendant that he deliver the plaintiff as good a gunn, if not the Same, with the money and Costs of suite.

Thomas Lovelace, Plaintiff
Cornelius Post,[101] Defendant. The 1st default.

Richard Lockwood,[102] Plaintiff
John Cavelier,[103] Defendant.
   The Plaintiff declared the defendant is indebted unto him for passage of his wife and Childe from Virginia to Boston the sume of forty shillings. The Court Orders Judgment to bee entred against the defendant with Cost.

Joseph Hedger,[104] Plaintiff
Albert Bush, Defendant. 1. Default.

Peter Smith,[105] Plaintiff
Margery Merritt,[106] Defendant.
    The Plaintiff by his Attorney declared that hee
    being indebted to the defendant f. 134 drew a bill
    upon C. Manning to pay the same, which was done
    accordingly, but notwithstanding in the said Capt.
    Manning's absence the defendant sued the plaintiff
    for the Said Summe and recovered it of him in the
    tyme of the Dutch Government, with Costs, with
    and by which unjust suite hee was damnified £5
    Sterling, wherefore prayes repayration, etc. The
    worshippfull Court having heard what both Parties
    could alleadge, and Mary Pallmer with Capt. Mann-
    ing to testifie the said debt was paid, They or-
    dered Judgment to bee entred against the defendant
    to Repay the principle unto the Plaintiff and to
    pay all Costs, both relating to the said matter.

Margery Merrit, Plaintiff
C. John Manning, Defendant.
    The worshippfull Court ordered a Nonsuite against
    the Defendant with Costs.

Hugo Barnson, Plaintiff
Daniell De Haert, Defendant.
    The Plaintiff's Attorney being ready to read his
    Declaration, the defendant desyred to have a Coppy
    of the declaration, which was granted him and or-
    dered to answer it the next Court day.

Anna Litscoe,[107] Plaintiff
Fred. De Drayer,[108] Defendant. 1. Default.

Tunis Crayes,[109] Plaintiff
Allard Anthony, Defendant. 1. Default.

William Sturt,[110] Plaintiff
John Tudor, Defendant.
    The Court order if they cannot agree by next Court,
    then to issue it.

Wessell Wessells,[111] Plaintiff
Arian Isackson & his Wife, Defendants.
    Mr. Cooke, the Plaintiff's attorney, declared that
    the plaintiff found the defendants' breaking open
    his chamber dore, etc. The Court ordered them to
    appeare to answer it the next court day.

Thomas Gibbs, Plaintiff
Otto Gerritz, Defendant. 1 Default.

Thomas Gibbs, Plaintiff
Arian Isackson & wife, Defendants.
   The Sherriff Presented the defendants for fighting
and breaking the kings peace, etc. The Court order to take the said matter into their consideration next Court day.

John Sharpe, Plaintiff
John Rider, Defendant.
   The plaintiff moved for Execution against the defendant upon a Judgment formerly granted. The
Court order the defendant to bring in his reasons
why Execution Shall not bee granted against him,
otherwise it shall be issued out accordingly.

Thomas De Lavall,[112] Plaintiff
Martine Mayor,[113] Defendant.
   The defendant is ordered to answer it next Court,
and the plaintiff's Agent to put in his declaration in writing to the end the defendant may have
a Coppy thereof & answer it.

Thomas Gibbs, Plaintiff
John Archer,[114] Defendant.
   The defendant making a default, the Court Order
to give him notice that if hee shew not reasons
why Execution shall not goe against him against
the next court it shall bee exhibited Accordingly.

The Sherriff, Plaintiff
Jacob Kipp,[115] Defendant.
   The Sherriff Presented the defendant for refusing
to obey the orders of the 3 Constables, giveing
them ill Language, saying hee would not bee ruled
by a company of fooles, etc. The defendant utter-
ly disowned the Charge. The Court order him to
give the Constables Civill satisfaction.

Jaculyne Turneur, Plaintiff
Eliz. Nachtigale, Defendant.
   The defendant brought into the Court her Suplica-
tory petition, in which was her acknowledgment for
her wrong and injury to the plaintiff's husband,
which the Court accepted off, conditionally she
behaved her Selfe well, and pay all costs.

This day the officers of Haerlam were Sworne which
were as followeth: David De Marey,[116] Constable; Cornelis Janson,[117] Jost Van Oblinus,[118] John Dyckman,[119]
Addolph. Mayor,[120] Overseers.

At an Espetiall Court held In New Yorke the 28 January 1674/5 At the Motion and Charge of Mr. Nicolas De
Mayor. Present: Mr. Mayor, Mr. Deputy, Mr. Phillipps,

Mr. Minviele, Mr. Winder.
    Capt. William Dyre, Attorney to
        Mr. Joseph and John Grafton of Salem in New
        England, Merchants, Plaintiff
    Mr. Nicholas De Mayor,[121] Defendant.
        The Plaintiff having atached a Ketch called the
        hope alias hopwell, formerly belonging to the said
        Graftons the returne thereof was read in Court.
        The Court queried whether it was admittable for 2
        Inhabitants to call a Speciall Court against each
        other; upon debate it was concluded Not unless
        upon Extraordinary Occasions.
        George Cooke, Attorney for the Defendant, brought
        in a Paper by way of Complaint that the Plaintiff
        would not give his Clyent a Coppy of the Declara-
        tion and prayed a Nonsuite with Cost and £25
        dammage for Stopping the Ketche's voyage. At
        length Plaintiff and Defendant consented to joyne
        issue and the Jury Empannilled, who were: C.
        Silv. Sallisbury, Mr. Ed. Dyer, Mr. Wm. Radney,
        Mr. Roger Rugg, Mr. Samuell Edsall, Mr. Nath.
        Spratt, Mr. Tho. Coker,[122] Mr. Jos. Knott,[124] Mr.
        Co. V Bursen,[125] Mr. Dan. De Harte, Mr. Pet.
        Jacobs, Mr. John Josten. John Rider, Attorney for
        the Plaintiff, read the declaration that the said
        Kech was unlawfully taken and not'lawfully con-
        demned, etc., and produced his Letter of Attorney,
        attested by 2 wittnesses viva voce, whereupon the
        defendant at his motion had ½ howers tyme given
        him to peruse and answer the Declaration, which
        hee did accordingly and brought it in. Then the
        bill of sale was read. Mr. Cooke, Attorney for
        the Defendant, brought in Governor Colve's bill of
        Sale and the Act of confiscation, Which, when the
        Court had heard what both parties could alleadge
        and all the papers read On boath sides, the Presi-
        dent gave the Charge to the Jury, who went out up-
        on their verdict & after Long debate brought in a
        Speciall verdict, which was as followeth, vizt.
        If a Councell of warr without Commission from
        either Prince of Orange or States of Holland, held
        in New Yorke, bee a Legall and Lawfull Court of
        Admiralty or Judicature, then the Jurors find for
        the defendant, But if such Councell of warr bee
        noe free Sollid and Leagall Court of Admiralty or
        Judicature, then the Jurors find for the Plaintiff
        and that the defendant doe forthwith deliver the
        vessell, paying Costs of Suite. The Defendant
        hereupon desyring an Appeale from the verdict of
        the Jury to his honnour the Governor, The Wor-
        shippfull Court haveing maturly pondered the Con-
        tents of the Espetiall verdict and Appeale, al-
        though both parties afterwards moved for the Judg-
        ment of the Court, they thought it most meete to

referr it to his honnour the Governour as was
first desyred. After which his honnour the Governour remitted the said refferrence back Againe
to the Mayor and Aldermen by his Speciall warrant,
requiring them to pass their Judgments thereupon
according to Law. In pursuance of which Order
the Court Satt on the 2d. February following and
after mature and deliberate debate & consultation
of the matter, the[y] finde that the vessell in
Controversye was taken in tyme of warr & in tyme
of warr was confiscated and Condemned, the Dutch
Governour being then personally present at the
said confiscation and Condemnation, who had the
sole power of the then Government, and doe Judge
the said matter to bee comprehended in our honnoured Governour's Proclamation, Confirming all
Legall Juditious proceedings, Therefore doe Order
Judgment to bee entred for the Defendant and the
plaintiff to pay ordinary Costs of suite. The
Plaintiff thereupon moved the Court for an Appeale to
to his honnour the Governour and Councell, which
Appeale is allowed according to Law.

At a Mayors Court held in New York the 9th of February 1674/5.

Present: Mr. Mathias Nicolls, Mayor; Mr. John Lawrence, Deputy; Mr. Fred. Phillipps, Mr. John Winder,
Aldermen.

Thomas Lovlace, Plaintiff
Samuell Rescoe, Defendant.
>The matter being by former Order referr'd to arbi-
trators, and before it cold bee determined, one of
the Elected Arbitrators was dead, wherefore the
Court by consent of both parties have ordered that
they make a new Election against next Court day,
otherwise the Court will determine it.

Tho. Lovlace, Plaintiff
Cornelius Post, Defendant.
>The defendant making a default, the Court order it
to bee suspended till next Court.

Walter Webley, Plaintiff
Mart Cregier, Defendant.
>The defendant making default, the Court order that
the former Judgment shall bee attended.

Walter Webley, Plaintiff
Abell Hardenbrooke,[126] Defendant.
>The Plaintiff declares for f. 200 wampom or the
value in wheate; the defendant produced a bill of
the plaintiff's for f.   , which the [sic] hee
sayes hee hath satisfied. The Court order Judgment to bee entred against the defendant for the
summe due on ballance and Costs of suite.

Olave Steevens, Plaintiff
C. John Manning, Defendant.
    The Plaintiff declared that the defendant was In
his debt in the summe of f. 631 seawants value,
which Summe the plaintiff atached in the hands of
Nicolas Bayard, and prayes Judgment. The defendant did not appeare, wherefore the Court ordered
if the defendant did not appeare the next court
day, then Judgment to pass against him.

Alice Manning, Plaintiff
Kath. Harrison, Defendant.
    The Plaintiff declares in an acction of Defama-
tion. The Court, haveing heard what both parties
could aleadge, at their request and by consent
referred it to the report of Doctor Taylor,[127]
otherwise to the Court will determine it the next
Court day.

Mr. Gabriell Minviele, Plaintiff
Claus Lock, Defendant.
    By consent of both parties the Court order this
acction to bee suspended.

Cornelis Corsen, Plaintiff
Arian Cornelis, Defendant.
    The Plaintiff's Default.

Joseph Hedger, Plaintiff
Albert Bush, Defendant.
    The Plaintiff declared the defendant deteyned a
gunn of his and about f. 12 seawant. The Court
ordered Judgment to bee entred against the defendant to restore the said gunn or one as good, with
the money and Costs of suite.

Hugo Barnson, Plaintiff
Daniell De Haert, Defendant.
    The plaintiff declaring in an acction of account,
the Defendant, alleaging the plaintiff was not
Capable of answering costs and dammages, moved the
Court that hee put in security before any further
proceedings, which the Court Ordered to bee done
accordingly and to trye the matter next Court day
by a Jury.

Anna Litscoe, Plaintiff
Fred. De Drayer, Defendant.
    The Plaintiff declared for f. 69.12 wampoms value.
The defendant making a default, the Court order
Judgment against the defendant with Costs of suite.

Tunis Cray, Plaintiff
Allard Anthony, Defendant
    The defendant default.

Anna Elizabeth Wessells,[128] Plaintiff
Ram Janson,[129] Defendant
    The plaintiff declared in an acction upon the Case
    for engaging his house to her and hath not per-
    formed the same to her dammage £ 25:00:0. Sterling
    and prayes a confirmation of the said Agreement or
    the Dammage. Roloph Janson,[130] Albert Bush & Ger-
    rardus Wessell brought their Evidences in writing
    to confirme the same; Allard Anthony, being sick,
    sent in a Petition to the court alleaging the de-
    fendant Lett the said house to him; John Shacker-
    ly allsoe made Clayme to the said house as hyred
    to him. The Court doe Order the parties to fitt
    themselves against the next Court day to try it by
    a Jury.

John Sharpe, Plaintiff
John Rider, Defendant
    The Plaintiff pressing the Court for Execution up-
    on a Judgment passed neare 20 moneths agoe against
    the defendant.

Wessell Wessells, Plaintiff
Arian Isaxon, Defendant
    The plaintiff default.

John Sharpe, Plaintiff
Executors of John Garland,[132] Defendants,
        vizt. Fr. Rumbouts[133] & Gelyne Verplanck[134]
    Gelyne appeared & disowned they were Executors but
    Mr. Rumbolt default.

Sherriff Gibbs, Plaintiff
Arian Isackon & wife, Defendants
    The Court order the defendants to agree with the
    sherriff & pay Costs.

Arian Isackson, Plaintiff
Wessell Wessells, Plaintiff
    The Court order this to bee referred untill next
    Court day. Defendant default.

Edward Dyer, Plaintiff
Martine Mayor, Defendant
    The Court order the Defendant to take out a Coppy
    of the declaration against next Court.

Sherriff Gibbs, Plaintiff
Otto Gerritson, Defendant
    The plaintiff presented the defendant for tapping

without a Lycence;   the court ordered Judgment
against the defendant that hee pay his fine to the
sherriff according as in the Law is exprest and
Costs of Court.

Thomas Gibbs, Plaintiff
John Archer, Defendant
    The Plaintiff moves for Execution upon a former
    Judgment. This Court confirmes the former Judg-
    ment and Costs.

Mr. John Lawrence, Plaintiff
Nicolas Bayard, Defendant
    The plaintiff declares for that the defendant had
    sold cartaine of his goods at ½ price which were
    violently and forceably taken from him in the
    tyme of the Dutch Government and prayes restora-
    tion and repayration of the Same with Costs. The
    worshippfull Court order the Parties to fitt them-
    selves for a tryall by a Jury the next Court day.

James Mathewes,[135] Plaintiff
Nicolas Bayard, Defendant
    The Court order to appoynt some persons to view
    the bookes.

Nicolas Bayard, Plaintiff
James Mathewes, Defendant
    The Court order this acction to bee suspended
    untill the next Court.

Anna Eliz. Wessells, Plaintiff
Thomas Taylor, Defendant
    The Plaintiff declares that the defendant is in-
    debted unto her f. 418. The defendant not appear-
    ing, the Court order if hee shew not reasons to
    the contrary next court day then Judgment shall
    bee granted against him.

John Sharpe, Plaintiff
Tho. Taylor, Defendant
    The Plaintiff moves for Execution upon the former
    Judgment. The Court order it Accordingly if the
    defendant shew not reasons against the next court
    day.

Francis Rumbolt, Plaintiff
John Speiglaer,[136] Defendant
    The plaintiff declares for f. 117.4. The defen-
    dant is ordered to shew reasons next court, other-
    wise Judgment to bee entred against him.

Order for the fines in default of Watching
    The affaire concerning the Publique watch of the

towne being taken into consideration by the Court of
Mayor and Aldermen this day by order of the Governour,
it is agreed upon & Ordered that every man in the list
of the 4 Companies delivered in by the Provost Shall
pay their defaults according to Custome, that is to say
2s. per tyme for every neglect of their duty without
respect of persons & the watch to continue as it now is
untill further order, and in case of refusall of payment by any of the persons within named the Constables
are hereby impowered to distreyne for the same. New
Yorke January 5th 1674/5.

    Isack Van Vleck,[137] Plaintiff
    Jan Speiglaer's wife,[138] Defendant
        The plaintiff declares for f. 139 sewant; the
        Court order the defendant to shew reasons the
        next court day why Judgment shall not pass
        against her; otherwise it shall be granted.

    Thomas Lewis,[139] Plaintiff
    Nelis Mathiason,[140] Defendant
        The Plaintiff declared the defendant had Broken
        his Covenant in not goeing upon his Land, etc.
        The Court order that the defendant take out a
        Coppy of the plaintiff's declaration in order to
        come to tryall next Court.

    Gerrit Hendrixon,[141] Plaintiff
    John Rider, Defendant
        The Plaintiff declared the defendant is indebted
        to him in the Summe of f.   . The Court or-
        der, if the defendant shew not reason to the con-
        trary next court day, Judgment Shall bee granted
        against him.

    Hump. Davenport, Plaintiff
    Francis Leigh,[142] Defendant
        The plaintiff declares the defendant is indebted
        unto him for rent f. 150; the Court orders Judg-
        ment to bee entred against the defendant with
        Costs.

    Sherriff Gibbs, Plaintiff
    Jacob Kipp, Defendant
        The Plaintiff presenteth the defendant for work-
        ing with his Mill on the Lord's day. The Court
        order that the defendant doe satisfye the fine to
        the Sherriff according to Law and Costs of the
        presentment.

    Sherriff Gibbs, Plaintiff
    Mrs. Poole, Defendant
        The Plaintiff presenteth the defendant for that
        shee draweth drinke and tappes without a Lycence.

The Worshippfull Court doe Order shee shall pay
her fine to the sherriff According to Law and
Costs of the presentment.

John Henry, Plaintiff
Jan Smedes, Defendant
   The Plaintiff moves the Court for Execution
   against the defendant upon a Judgment formerly
   granted; the Court orders the former Judgment to
   bee attended.

At an Extraordinary meeting at the towne hall in New
Yorke On the 19th February 1674/5.
   Present: His Honnour the Governour; Mr. Mathias
Nicolls, Mayor; Mr. Deputy Mayor; Mr. Fred. Phillipps,
Alderman; Mr. John Winder, Alderman.
   His Honnour the Governour Laying open the great ne-
cessity of the Diamond Friggott's being speedely suplied
with her Proportion of Bisquet for her voyadge to Europe,
the 4 Eminenst Bakers of this Cityy were sent for, who
tendred to bake soe much as their Corne would afford at
16 per lb. if paid in Silver or Beaver. Mr. Samuell
Griffith for and on the behalfe of Capt. Griffith tendred to pay the said Bakers fifteene shillings in Silver
or Beaver for each hundred weight, upon which the said
Bakers were appoynted to goe and consult about the matter and bring their report to the Mayor at 2 of the
Clocke in the afternoone, who did accordingly and under-
writt their portions to Supply the said friggot with
15000 pounds.
   His honnour the Governour having committed Peter Janson Meade to the Prison of this Citty for having taken
into his house an Iron Stove and sundry other moveables
belonging to the fort and deteyning and concealing the
same contrary to the Proclamation made and publisht to
prevent such abuses, the Sherriff thereupon presented
the said Peter Janson, who upon Examination produced a
Certificate under the hands of 2 of the Dutch officers
that they gave or sold the premisses. The honnourable
Governour out of favour to the Delinquent tooke noe
notice of the other moveables, only the Iron Stove.
Whereupon the Worshippfull Court doe order that the said
Peter Janson Meade Shall send the said Stove into the
fort againe and cause it to bee sett upp in the same
place from whence it was taken away and in the same Condition at his owne propper Charge and that hee pay to
the sherriff the summe of f. 40 Gelders to bee disposed
of at the Court's Pleasure, as alsoe that hee Petition
the honnoured Governour for Excuse and pardon of his
fault and pay the Costs of his presentment and imprison-
ment.

Mr. Sherriff, Complainant
Cornelis the fisher,[143] Defendant
    The sheriff presented Cornelis the fisher for
    strowing seditious words against the peace of his
    Majestie and the welfare of this Government. The
    worshippfull Court doe Order that the said Cor-
    nelis the fisher doe enter into a recognizance
    for his good behaviour and for his appearance when
    required, which was done accordingly.

Sherriff Gibbs, Complainant
David Ogden, Defendant
    The sheriff Presented David Ogden for strowing
    abroad seditious rumours and reports about the
    country, who alleaged that Cornelis the Fisher
    was the person heard to Speake the said words and
    avered the same before him. Whereupon the Wor-
    shippfull Court Ordered that the said Ogden doe
    enter into a recognizance to Our Soveraigne Lord
    the King for the summe of Twenty pounds to appeare
    in person before the honnourable Governour to
    avere and give testimony against the said Cornelis
    the Fisher for the said Matter, the said Ogden to
    put in security allsoe which hee did by Mathias
    De Haert accordingly.
    Whereas Arian Cornelison does Avere and affirme
    that one Peter the Scott did say unto Joannes
    Cowenhoven[144] that the Dutch enemy were seene to
    Clyme upp the fort walls and that the Said Scott
    was then a Centinell and see the King's flagg
    struck and the Prince's Flagg hoysted upp and that
    the English soldiers cryed for Quarter with much
    more such Like reports. Whereupon the Worshipp-
    full Court ordered that the said Arian Cornelison
    doe enter into a recognizance for the Summe of
    Twenty Pounds that hee shall appeare to prosecute
    what is alleadged against the said Scott. And the
    said Arian Cornelison standeth bound for Castian
    Castianson to the Same effect whensoever the
    honnourable Governour Or the authority Shall re-
    quire it, which was done accordingly.

The Court adjourned.

At an Extraordinary meeting of Mayor & Aldermen at
the Towne Hall the 6 of March 1674/5.
    Present: Mr. Mathias Nicolls, Mayor; Mr. Deputy
Mayor; Mr. Fre. Phillipps, Mr. Gabr. Minviele, Mr. John
Winder, Aldermen.
    Proclamation. The Worshippfull Court Ordered that
the Proclamation for the Continuation of the imbargoe of
Wheate or meale unbolted from this Port bee Continued
untill the Moneth of October next, which was before the
Towne Published accordingly.

Proclamation. The Proclamation for the due observation of the Sabboth was this day Published, with the Renovation & confirmation thereof.

Proclamation. Alsoe the Proclamation for the Bakers to observe the former Orders about the keeping wheate and Rye bread in their shopps for the supply of the Inhabitants and the weight thereof to bee as therein is specefied on the Penalties therein mentoned.

Proclamation. Alsoe forbidding all persons from taking away any boates or Canewes from any place within this Government according to the Contents of the former Proclamation made and Published for that purpose.

The Confirmation of Mr. Christopher Hoghland[145] in the office of Surveyor and Brander of Bread and flower, And Richard Ellott[146] Surveyor and Packer of Beefe and Porke, and Swore in his office.

Done publiquly at the Towne Hall.

The Governour and Councell's Order was this day Published to reinforce the Lawe Concerning forbidding any Ballast to be throwne overboard in any of the Harbours, Rhoades or Ryding places within this Government on the penalties therein mentioned.

Upon Complaint of Mr. Lee, haven Master of this Citty, that by meanes of many loades of Stones which lye on the shoare syde Boates and Vessells are mutch damnified by the same and hindred from Comming neare to land their goods, wherefore the Court have ordered the said Mr. Lee to see the same taken up and the strand cleared as much as possibly hee cann And in order thereunto the Court doe require the Carmen of this Citty to bee assistant to the said Mr. Lee and to bring the said stones where hee shall appoynt not farr from the waterside And care shall bee taken for their payment.

At a Court held in New Yorke the 8th day of March 1674/5.

Present: C. Mathias Nicols, Mayor; Mr. John Lawrence, Deputy; Mr. Fred. Phillipps, Mr. John Winder, Aldermen.

Tho. Lovlace, Plaintiff
Samuell Rescoe, Defendant
    The worshippfull Court order to make a Definitive determination of this Cause next Court day.

Tho. Lovlace, Plaintiff
Cornelius Post, Defendant
    The Court order that an end bee made of this action next court day if the Parties doe not agree among themselves.
March 8th 1674/5.

Mr. John Lawrence, Plaintiff
Nicolaus Bayard, Defendant
    The plaintiff declares in acction of the Case as

per his Declaration. The defendant read his answer and Soe replickt and duplickt, upon which a Jury was empannelled, who were as followeth: C. Humphry Davenport, Mr. Roger Rugg, Mr. Josias Jonson, Mr. Tho. Lewis, Mr. Nath. Spratt, Mr. Joseph Lee. Lowr. Van Derspeigle,[148] Peter Jacobs, Corn. Van Bursen, Reynier Williamson,[149] Luycas Tienhoven, Timo. Gabriells.[150] And after both parties had maturly made good their Pleas and Wittnesses on boath sides heard and sworne the Worshippfull Mayor gave them their Charge and after Long debate brought in their verdict as followeth: The Jury finds the Fiscall's Proceedings against the Plaintiff was illegall, and therefore wee find for the Plaintiff and that the defendant forthwith returne the goods or the value of them to the Plaintiff for his goods soe onjustly taken away according to declaration, with Costs of suite. Whereupon the defendant motioned an Appeale from the Jurye's verdict.

Hugo Barnson, Plaintiff
Daniell De Haert, Defendant
The Worshippfull Court finding the plaintiff's Plea and acction vexatious and noe probabillity to satisfye dammages doe order the cause to bee Struck of the Docket and the plaintiff to pay Costs.

Walter Webly, Plaintiff
C. Mart. Cregier, Defendant
The Court order Judgment to bee entred against the defendant that hee make good and restore unto the plaintiff all the goods hee hath in trust, Only those which were taken from him when the Governour was present, and the defendant to pay costs.

Alice Manning, Plaintiff
Catherne Harrison, Defendant
The Plaintiff declared on an acction of Defamation and the Court having heard what both parties could alleadge and prove, they ordered that the defendant doe at the next mayors Court make a Publique accknowledgment of the wrong done to the Plaintiff and pay Costs of suite.

Lady Esabella Stross, Plaintiff
Katherne Harrison, Defendant
The Plaintiff declared for certaine goods of hers deteyned by the defendant, and the Court, having heard what both parties cold alleage, doe order Judgment to bee entred against the defendant that

shee doe speedely restore and deliver unto the
plaintiff all such things as were Left in trust
in her hands and what else can bee proved she had
in her Posession of the Plaintiff's and pay Costs
of suite, the proofe to bee made by Mrs. Hawkins,[151] Mrs. Johns[152] or any Other Credible per-
son, or if any of the said goods are disposed of
then the defendant is to pay the equivalent value
of them.

Olave Stephens Van Cortland, Plaintiff
Capt. John Manning, Defendant
    The Parties not being ready, the Court doe order
    this cause to bee heard next Court day.

Gabriell Minviele, Plaintiff
Claus Lock, Defendant
    The Court doe order the 2 former Arbitrators to
    agree and compose the matter amongst themselves
    if possible, Otherwise to Chuse a third person
    for an Umpire.

Cornelis Corsen, Plaintiff
Arian Cornelis, Defendant
    The Court doe order Judgment to bee entred against
    the defendant that hee deliver the Servant to the
    plaintiff with Costs. Principle £ 4:10:0.

Searjeant Tho. Ashton,[153] Plaintiff
Samuell Willson,[154] Defendant
    The Court Orders both parties to bee ready to have
    the matter determined next Court day.

The Court adjourned till 2 of the Clock in the
afternoone.

John Sharpe, Plaintiff
Thomas Taylor, Defendant
    The defendant not appearing with his reasons to
    prevent Execution according to the former Court's
    order, the Court doe give order and Grant Execu-
    tion against the defendant, upon the former Judg-
    ment.

Lawrence Vander Spiegle, Plaintiff
Mrs. Elizabeth Bedloo, Defendant
    The Plaintiff producing his declaration which was
    brought into the Court in due tyme and his account
    therewith, the defendant's son, Mr. John Shacker-
    ley, moved the Court for Coppie thereof against
    next Court, which was granted and Ordered accord-
    ingly.

Tunis Crayes, Plaintiff
Allard Anthony, Defendant
    Upon the Petition of the Plaintiff that former
    Courts ordered Judgments against the defendant to
    pay him f. 418 for victualling certaine Prisoners
    that were imprisoned in the Goale of this Citty,
    it being made appeare by Coppies thereof, this
    Worshippfull Court confirmed the said Judgments
    and ordered that if the defendant shew not reason
    to the contrary against next court day Execution
    shall issue out against him.

Anna Eliza. Wessells, Plaintiff
Thomas Taylor, Defendant
    The plaintiff declared for f. 418 due to her per
    account. The defendant not appearing, the Court
    ordered Judgment to bee entred against him by de-
    fault with Costs.

Henry Van Dyke, Plaintiff
Allard Anthony, Defendant
    Both defaulted.

Thomas Lewis, Plaintiff
Nelis Matyson, Defendant
    The defendant not appearing, the Court Ordered if
    hee did not appeare next court day Judgment should
    bee granted against him.

James Mathewes, Plaintiff
Nicolaus Bayard, Defendant
                    &
Nicolas Bayard, Plaintiff
James Mathewes, Defendant
    The Court doe order these Acctions to bee suspend-
    ed till next Court.

Abell Hardenbrooke, Plaintiff
Antonio De Milt,[155] Defendant
    The Plaintiff read his declaration and the Court
    having what both parties cold alleadge did order
    the rest due to the defendant from the Plaintiff
    should bee acquitted by reason they conceived Soe
    great a Summe for a fine to the Schout was too un-
    reasonable and that the defendant doe pay Mr. New-
    ton the former fees due to him, and each to pay
    his owne costs of this suite.

Robert Hollis, Plaintiff
Tho. Hatfeild, Defendant
    Both making default, the Court ordered this
    action to bee suspended till next Court day.

Anna Wessells, Plaintiff
Ram. Johnson, Defendant
   The Court doe order both partyes to bee ready for
   a tryall by a Jury against the next Court day.

Elias Doughty,[156] Plaintiff
Eliz. Bedloo, Defendant
   The Court order the defendant to take out a Coppy
   of the declaration in order to come to tryall the
   next Court.

Elias Doughty, Plaintiff
Derrick Smith,[157] Defendant
   The Plaintiff declared for £ 150 Boston money due
   to him for the halfe of Yonker Vander Duncks[158]
   Land and Mill. The debt being proved, and both
   parties heard, the Court doe order that Judgment
   bee entred against the defendant that hee pay the
   said summe with the interest in 4 moneths and
   Costs of suite, Only to discount what is paid and
   put in security to the plaintiff's Liking for per-
   formance of the Same.

Mattyas Evertz, Plaintiff
Dirrick Smith, Defendant
   The Plaintiff declared for f. 287 due to him and
   proved the same. The Court order Judgment against
   the defendant, with Costs, Only deducting 8s. for
   a gallon of Brandy he hath had.

John Sharpe, Plaintiff
John Rider,[159] Defendant
   The Court finding the former Judgment to bee good,
   doe approve and Confirme the same and order the
   defendant to pay the plaintiff the said summe of
   f. 483.10 with Interest for the same from the tyme
   of the first Judgment, and all Costs of suite
   within two monethes, Otherwise Execution to bee
   issued out against him for the same.

Gerrit Hendrix, Plaintiff
John Rider, Defendant
   The parties declaring they are upon agreement, the
   Court order this acction to bee suspended till the
   next Court day.

Isack Van Vleck,[160] Plaintiff
Gerrit Spieglaer, Defendant
   The Plaintiff demands f. 185. The Court orders
   hee shall prove hee delivered the Ancor annys,
   otherwise to pay costs and if hee prove the de-
   livery then the defendant is to pay the debt and
   Costs.

Nicolaus Bayard, Plaintiff
John Rider, Defendant
   The Court order the defendant to take out a Coppy
   of the plaintiff's declaration to bee ready for a
   tryall next Court day.

John Williams,[161] Plaintiff
Hartmann Wessells,[162] Defendant
   The Plaintiff declares for £2.13.0. due to him.
   The Court orders that the defendant shew reasons
   to the Contrary next Court, Otherwise they will
   pass Judgment against him.

Jacob Lenderson,[163] Plaintiff
Jan Tunison,[164] Defendant
   Parties not being ready, the Court order to suspend it till next Court day if they doe not in
   the meane tyme compose it.

Dirrick Evertz,[165] Plaintiff
John Blackwell, Defendant
   The Plaintiff declared hee had layd out and dis-
   bursted severall monys for the defendant. The
   Court having heard what both parties cold alleage
   Ordered the defendant to pay the Plaintiff his
   just due, and Costs of suite.

Elizab. Nachtingale, Plaintiff
Widdow Turneur, Defendant
   The defendant appearing and the plaintiff default,
   the court finding it a vexatious suite doe Order
   a Nonsuite against the Plaintiff and pay Costs.

Wessell Wessells, Plaintiff
Arian Isackson, Defendant
                    &
Arian Isackson, Plaintiff
Wessell Wessells, Defendant
   The Court finding both these acctions Letidgious
   doe order them to bee put out of the List and
   each to pay the Costs of his owne acction.

Sherriff Gibbs, Complainant
Jacob Vande Water,[166] Defendant
   The Sherriff presenteth the defendant for taking
   skins from Indians on purpose to force them to
   sell them to him and noe other, hee Excusing him-
   selfe with Submission to the Court, they pass by
   his fault but order that hee pay the Costs.

Mrs. Susanna Garland.[167] Petitions the Court to
   grant her Letters of Administration who complyed
   therewith and order her to bring in a true inventary of all her husband's estate Against next

Court day.

Mrs. Johns.[168] Petitions the Court for the Like,
which was granted accordingly, and shee alsoe ordered to bring in a true inventary of her husband's estate the next Court.

The Court broke up.

At a Court Meeting held on Saturday the 13th March
1674/5.
Present: Mr. Mathias Nicolls, Mayor; Mr. John Lawrence, Deputy; Mr. Fre. Phillips, Mr. Gabriell Minviele, Mr. John Winder, Aldermen.
Proclamation. This day the Governour's order was
publisht at the towne hall for all Such persons as doe
intend to continue within this his R H Government and
Live under his Majestie's Obedience, they shall take the
usuall oathes of Allegiance and fidellity which is appoynted to Begin on Munday next, at the bell ringing,
which shall bee a warning to them to give their attend-
ance theron.
The Governour's Order alsoe was Publist forbidding
and prohibiting all forreiners and Strangers or Others
to trade within his Ro H territories without comming to
this port and there to make their due entries according
to Law, under the penalties therein mentioned.

At a Court Meeting held on Munday the 15 of March
1674/5.
Present: All but Mr. Darvall.
Mr. Corn. Stenwyck,[169] Mr. Egidias Luyke, Mr. W.
Beekman, Mr. Jacob Kipp, Mr. Joannes Van Brughen, Mr.
Joannes De Piester, Mr. Antony De Milt, Mr. Nicolas
Bayard And divers others who as head or Speakers for the
rest came into the Court and desired a Confirmation of
their former priviledges granted to them by Governour
Nicolls. The President demanding what they were, they
replyed:
    1. To have the Liberty of the Church,
    2. That their people shall not bee Prest,
    3. That the Article of inherritance bee confirm-
ed,
    4. That they shall not bee oblidged to take up
Armes against their owne Nation.
All which they requested the Court to recommend to the
Governour before they take the Oath, upon which the
Court went and accquainted his Honnour therewith, who by
the advice of his Councell gave them the answer following: That without Condition, Articles or Provisoes they
must take the Oath. Otherwise to stand to the Censure &
penalty in the Lawes sett forth.

At a Court Meeting on Wednesday the 17th March 1674/5.

Present: All but Mr. Wm. Darvall.

The forementioned persons delivered to the Court a Petition to intercede with his honnour the Governour on behalfe of their Priviledges. Mr. Cornelis Steenwyck proposes to have 24 howers to Consider of it before hee take the Oath. Mr. Bayard desired some competent tyme to dispose of their estates and depart, and requests an answer to the Later part of their petition which hath relation to the 9 Article that that they shall not bee prest to fight against their owne nation.

Mr. Mayor. Hee Cold say nothing thereof having noe order from the Governour about it, Whereupon Mr. Paulus Richards[170] desyred to take his Oath, & was sworne accordingly.

> Capt. Wm. Dyre presented a Petition to the Court to grant him a writt of appraizment for a Certaine parcell of Beavers, Peltry and Tobaccoe, Seized and found on board the shipp Exchange of Amsterdam, the owners of which goods hath not his Majestie's Customes. Three of the shipps officers brought in a Petition to the Court that said Beavers & peltry might bee restored to them being theirs, and were Examined upon severall interogations.

Referr to day blotter No. A for a more full order heere Ommitted. 140 Sworne. Foure and forty of the Cittysens were this day Sworne the Oath of Fidellity, their names being in the Court day booke No. A.

18 March 117 sworne. One hundred & seaventeene Cittysens were this day sworne.

19 March 76 sworne. Seaventy Six sworne this day.

23 March 44 sworne. forty four sworne this day.

25.26 March 33 sworne. Thirty three sworne this day.

March 19th 1674/5.

Proclamation. This day was published a Proclamation to informe the people that the Court would attend this weeke and the next to receive the Oaths of fidellity and allegeance, and on Court dayes for persons absent On Court dayes.

Proclamation. Allsoe the Proclamation that all persons who are true subject to his Majestie and Royall highness shall give notice or information to his honnour the Governour or some of his Majestie's Justices of Peace Concerning all manner of Mutinous words or acctions they shall see or heare done or spoken Against Majestie, his R. Hyghnesse or the peace of this Government.

At a Mayors Court held in New Yorke 23d March 1674/5.
Present: Mr. Nicolls, Mayor;   Mr. Lawrence, Deputy;
Mr. Minviele, Mr. Phillipps, Aldermen.

Thomas Lovlace, Plaintiff
Samuell Rescoe, Defendant
> The Court order this acction to the refferrence
> of Mr. Roger Rugg and Mr. Daniell De Haert, who
> are desyred to make their report thereof next
> Court day.

Thomas Lovlace, Plaintiff
Cornelis Post, Defendant
> The Plaintiff declared for 1545 lbs. Tobaccoe.
> Both parties being heard, the court Order Judg-
> ment against the defendant for the said tobaccoe
> and Costs of suite.

Alice Manning, Plaintiff
Katherne Harrison, Defendant
> The Court having now heard the testimonye and
> allegations of Docter Taylor and taken the same
> into serious consideration, doe thinke fitt to
> reverse the former Judgment, finding it was a
> needless and vexatious suite, and therefore doe
> Order the Plaintiff to pay all Costs, and the de-
> fendant not to make any acknowledgment.

William Welch[171] & Francis Lee,[172] Porters, moved
> the Court to bee dismist from their Employs, which
> the Court granted.

Mathew Force Petitioned the Court to bee appoynted a
> Porter in one of their Steads and was accordingly
> admitted & sworne.

Anna Elizabeth Wessell, Plaintiff
Ram Johnson, Defendant
> A Jury was impanneled who were Mr. Roger Rugg, Mr.
> Sam. Blagg, Anto. Jenkins, Nath. Spratt, Josi.
> Johnson, Jam. Mathews, Hen. Bowman, Der. Van
> Cleyfe, Lawrence Vander Spiegle, Derrick Smith,
> Reynier Williamson, George Davis.[173]
> The Plaintiff declared in an acction of the Case
> for hyring or Letting to her a Certaine house in
> this Citty, and by not performing his Covenant
> shee is damnified £25 Sterling. The Court having
> heard what both parties Cold alleadge and the
> Wittnesses sworne, The President gave the charge
> to the Jury, who after Long and deliberate debate
> brought in their verdict for the Plaintiff and
> was as followeth.

Thomas Lewis, Plaintiff
Nelis Mattyson, Defendant
    The Plaintiff declared that the defendant had
    hyred a certaine parcell of Land, Meadow & other
    accommodations and did in noe wise performe his
    Covenant, by which hee was greatly damnified.
    The Covenant proved and the Case maturly heard,
    the Mayor gave the charge to the Jury, who went
    out & brought in their verdict for plaintiff,
    vizt.

Mr. Olave Stephens, Plaintiff
C. John Manning, Defendant
    The Court doe order that Pieter Jacobs and Assur
    Levy[174] doe bring in the Accounts of Capt. Mann-
    ing the next Court.

Tunis Craye, Plaintiff
Allard Antony, Defendant
    The Plaintiff declared for f. 442; both Parties
    being heard, the Court doe order Judgment against
    the defendant that if the f. 184 bee the whole
    debt that by the defendant alleaged, then the mat-
    ter is determined, but if it appeare otherwise
    that the Plaintiff hath f. 442 due to him, the
    defendant shall pay him the remainder with Costs
    of suite.

Robert Hollis, [175] Plaintiff
Tho. Hatfeild, Defendant
    The Plaintiff declared for f. 134 due to him. The
    Court order that if they doe not agree Judgment to
    to bee entred against the defendant with Costs.

Allard Antony, Plaintiff
Ram Johnson, Defendant
    The Court order this case to bee Suspended untill
    the acction betweene Eliz. Wessells and the defen-
    dant bee determined.

Elias Doughty, Plaintiff
Derrick Smith, Defendant
    The Plaintiff complaines against the defendant for
    that hee will not performe the former Judgment.
    The Court orders him forthwith to doe it, other-
    wise to grant an attachment upon his estate.

John Sharpe, Plaintiff
Wm. Bogardus,[176] Defendant
    The Plaintiff declared against the defendant for
    that hee is indebted to him for part of an Ox and
    Expenses the summe of f. 287.9 seawant. The de-
    fendant making 2 defaults, the Court order Judg-
    ment to bee passed against him that hee pay the

said summe with Costs of suite.

Jacob Leenderson, Plaintiff
Jan Tunison, Defendant
   Both parties making default, the Court ordered a
   Nonsuite against the plaintiff if hee appeare not
   to presente his acction the next Court.

Walter Webley, Plaintiff
Abell Hardenbrooke, defendant
   The Court haveing heard what both parties cold
   alleadge, Ordered that what the plaintiff is indebted to the man, it shall bee discounted, the
   defendant to pay the plaintiff the rest and Costs
   of suite.

Samuell Edsall, Plaintiff
Elizab. Poole, Defendant
   The Plaintiff declared that the defendant had
   drawne Liquors without paying duties. Shee not
   appearing, the Court Ordered that if shee shewes
   not reasons to the Contrary next Court, shee shall
   have her Lysence taken away and pay the fine, according as in the Law is sett forth.

Emanuell Mandevile,[177] Plaintiff
John Shackerley,[178] Defendant
   The Plaintiff declared that the defendant deteyned a Negro woman from him. The Court Orders that
   the atachmant stand fast, and the defendant not
   to deliver the Negro untill a decision bee made
   of the matter by the Court and a Jury, which if in
   a moneth there can bee tymly notice from Mr.
   George Hall.

Emanuell Mandevile, Plaintiff
Nicolas De Mayor, Defendant
   The Plaintiff's Attorney committing an Error in
   his declaration, the defendant demurred; thereupon the Court ordered the Plaintiff to mend his
   declaration and bee ready for tryall the next
   Court.

John Tuder, Plaintiff
Josia & Hannah Hellman,[179] Defendants
   The Plaintiff declared in an acction of Defamation
   and proved the same, whereupon the Court order
   that the defendant put in security to Prove her
   words in Six moneths.

George Davis, Plaintiff
Administrator of Anna Molyne, Defendant.
   The Plaintiff declared for 345 Carolus Guilders
   due to his wife from the said Anna Molyne. The

Court orders that the atachment continue on the
house and a Coppy of the declaration bee ready
for the defendant.

Henry Vandyke, Plaintiff
Allard Antony, Defendant
    The Court haveing heard this matter doe order that
    the defendant doe Speedely make up the fence that
    appertaines to him and good men to bee appoynted
    to view the dammage.

Capt. Casibulan Burton, Plaintiff
William Sturt,[180] Defendant
    The Plaintiff declares that the defendant is in-
    debted unto him for freight of goods. The Court
    desyred them to choose some good men to heare and
    determine the said matter and to make a Report
    thereof to the next Court.

Peter Aldrix, Plaintiff
Gerrit Hugo, Defendant
    The Plaintiff declared for f. 28.12 hallands money
    and 4 Beavers due to him from the defendant.
    Both parties being heard, the Court order Judg-
    ment against the defendant, that hee pay the said
    money and Beavers but if hee bring in a reason-
    able bill and the Court approve thereof, it shall
    bee allowed & discounted out of the said money
    and the defendant pay Costs.

Nicolas De Mayor, Plaintiff
Steentye Lowrence,[181] Defendant
    The Court order the defendant to take out a Coppie
    of the declaration & bee ready to joyne Issue the
    next Court.

Humphry Davenport, Plaintiff
Col. Fran. Lovlace, Defendant
    The Plaintiff declares for some Land taken from
    him by the defendant. The Court orders the matter
    to bee recommended to his honnour the Governour to
    doe therein as to his honnour shall seeme meete.

Searjeant Ashton,[182] Plaintiff
Samuell Willson, Defendant
    The Court having maturely heard what both parties
    Cold alleadge, did order Judgment against the de-
    fendant that hee pay the remainder due to the
    plaintiff and each beare the halfe of the Charge
    of Process.

Susanna Garland is ordered forthwith to bring in her
    inventary in order to her administration. Other-
    wise one of the Creditors shall doe it.

Dudley Lovlace,[183] Defendant
George Cooke,[184] Plaintiff
    The Plaintiff moved for a Confirmation of a Judg-
mant formerly Granted, which the Court Orders
accordingly.

Sherriff, Towne Clearke and Henry Newton[185] Complained that Frederick the drayer will not pay them
their fees, whereupon the Court Ordered Execution
to bee issued out against him for the same.

Collonell Lovelace his Estate. Upon the Governour's
order to this Court that the former attachment
bee prosecuted to Execution in order to which the
Estate of Collonell Lovlace shall bee Legally appraised. Wherefore the Court doe desyre and appoynt Mr. Samuell Edsall,[186] Mr. Thomas Lewis, Mr.
Adolph Pieterson[187] & Mr. Allard Antony to view
and value his estate in this Citty and to make
their report to this Court next Court day.

Brandmasters. The worshippfull Court finding it
very requesite and needefull to have brand Masters to
Looke after fowle Chimneys and fyers in this Citty according former Custome, doe nominate and appoynt Mr.
Evert Duyking and Mr. Henry Williamson, Bakers, to Execute & act therein as formerly & to Looke after the
Lathers, hookes & fyer Bucketts with Priviledges accustomary.

March 24 1675
Proclamacon about hoggs. This day was Proclaymed the
edict prohibiting hoggs goeing about the streets of this
Citty Longer then 8 dayes after the Publication, on the
penalty of f. 20 for the first offense, f. 40 for the
second, forfeiture of the hoggs found in the streets &
Seized for the third offense, and the Constables of this
Citty are ordered to see this edict put in Execution.
The hoggs soe seized are to bee disposed of at the ap-
poyntment of the Mayor or his Deputy.

Hugo Barnson, Plaintiff
Daniell De Haert, Defendant
    The court, taking Cognizance of the Insolvency of
the plaintiff, order that hee should not bee admitted to come to tryall unless hee did provide
security for the summe of £5 to pay costs and
dammages if hee makes not good his acction, whereupon the plaintiff brought his 2 sonns & entred
into bond for the summe of five Pounds as under
their hands in Court day booke No. A fol.: was
signed Gerit Huygen the Cleyne[188] & Leendert Huygen de Cleyne.[189]

At a Mayors Court held in New Yorke the 20th day of
Aprill 1675.
Present: Mr. Nicolls, Mayor; Mr. Lawrence, Deputy;
Mr. Phillipps, Mr. Minviele, Aldermen.

Thomas Lovlace, Plaintiff
Samuell Rescoe, Defendant
> Mr. Roger Rugg and Mr. Daniell De Haert brought
> in their report, which was sealed up. The Court
> read the same, which conteyned as followeth: wee
> whose names are here underwritten doe finde by
> the date and booke that the Last account given by
> Mr. Tho. Lovlace to the defendant of £10.16. & 7
> Bushells of Peaz is distinct from the first
> account of £53.6.4. Whereupon the Court ordered
> Judgment against the defendant for the said debt
> with Costs of suite.

Olave Steevens, Plaintiff
C. John Manning, Defendant
> The Court haveing heard what the plaintiff cold
> alleage thought it reasonable that his Claime
> should bee brought in with the rest of the Credi-
> tors when the defendant's debts are to bee paid
> and in the meane tyme the court order this
> acction to come noe more on the List.

Thomas Taylor, Plaintiff
Thomas Cornish,[190] Defendant
> The Plaintiff declared against the defendant for
> that hee by misinformacion obteyned his liberty
> from the duke's power to desert his Master's Ser-
> vice, by which hee is damnified £35 Sterling &
> prayes reparation. The Plaintiff having produced
> what papers and testimony hee had to prove his
> plea, which the Court read and heard, the defen-
> dant had the like Liberty, and after the Court
> had heard maturly what both parties cold alleage,
> the President gave the Jury their Charge, who
> went out and brought in their verdict as follow-
> eth: In the Case depending betweene Thomas Tay-
> lor, Plaintiff, and Thomas Cornish, defendant,
> the Jury find for the defendant with Costs. The
> Court order Judgment to bee entred against the
> Plaintiff with Costs.

Tunis Cray, Plaintiff
Allard Anthony, Defendant
> The worshippfull Court having heard what both
> parties cold alleage, they ordered that the plain-
> tiff bring in his account against next court.

Henry Vandyke, Plaintiff
Allard Anthony, Defendant
> In this Case the Court doe order that they doe

compose the said Matter if possible, otherwise to
determine it the next Court day.

Capt. Wm. Dyre, Plaintiff
Egidius Luyke, Defendant
    The Plaintiff on behalfe of his Royall Highness
declared in an acction of debt that hee the defendant is indebted unto Coll. Francis Lovlace in
the summe of f. 3317.15.8 in Beavers & f. 6319.15
seawant, as by two severall obligations. Both
appeare and all what cold bee alleadged on both
sides heard and papers read.

Thomas Lovlace, Plaintiff
Lucas Tienhoven, Defendant
    The Plaintiff declared that hee had a Judgment 4
yeares agoe against the defendant and an execution upon the Land. The Court seeing the matter
very just, doe order that if the defendant doe
not speedely pay it the Execution to bee renewed,
with Costs.

Antony Billopp
Tobias Aliston
    The defendant being Committed upon suspition of
fellony, none came in to accuse him. The Court
ordered to accquitt him, which was done accordingly.

The Court Adjourned untill 9 tomorrow morning.

At a Court held 21st Aprill 1675.
    Present: Mr. Nicolls, Mayor; Mr. Lawrence, Deputy;
Mr. Phillipps, Mr. Minviele, Aldermen.
    Emanuell Mandevile, Plaintiff
Nicol De Mayor, Defendant
    The Plaintiff's attorney read his declaration for
deteyning a negro belonging to Major Kingsland.[191]
All papers being read, wittnesses sworne and both
parties heard what cold bee alleaged, the Jury
had their Charge and went out and after mature debate brought in their verdict as followeth: The
Jury finds the negro man by name Arro to bee unjustly deteyned from him, the plaintiff, by the
defendant; therefore they finde for the plaintiff
and that the defendant forthwith deliver the said
negro man unto the Plaintiff according to declaration, with Costs of suite, Nath. Davenport. The
Court accepted of the verdict and ordered Judgment
to bee entred accordingly, with Costs.

Emanuell Mandevile, Plaintiff
John Shackerley, Defendant
    The Plaintiff declared against the defendant that

hee deteyned a Negro woman of his and proved her
to bee his negro. The Worshippfull Court haveing
heard the wittnesses, papers read and the debates
of both parties gave the Charge to the Jury, who
went out & brought in their verdict as followeth:
the Jury finds the Negro woman by name Ezebetha
to be unjustly deteyned by the defendant from the
Plaintiff. Therefore wee finde for the Plaintiff
and that the defendant deliver the said Negro unto the plaintiff according to declaration with
Costs of suite. Nathaniell Davenport. Whereupon
the Court accepted of the verdict but ordered
Judgment to bee suspended untill farther Order.

Arian Isackson, Plaintiff
Wessell Wessells, defendant
    Mr. Leete,[192] the Plaintiff's Attorney read the
    declaration. The Court conceiving the acction is
    needless and vexatious, ordered the defendant to
    put in Security to pay Cost and dammages if Cast,
    whereupon Timotheus Gabry tendred himselfe to bee
    his security to prove the acction or pay Costs
    and dammages and entred into a ten pound recogni-
    zance before the Court accordingly, and the Cause
    to bee tryed by a Jury next Court.

Joseph Harrison, Plaintiff
Vrian Plancke, Defendant
    The Court, haveing the debates of both parties,
    doe order the defendant to pay the Plaintiff f.30
    or what is due to him with Costs.

Abell Hardenbrooke, Plaintiff
Elizabeth Dumb, Defendant
    The Plaintiff declared that the defendant is in-
    debted unto him in the summe of f. 371. The Court
    orders that Judgment bee entred against the defen-
    dant for the said summe, with intrest & Costs.

Mr. John Lawrence, Plaintiff
Nicolas Bayard, Defendant
    On the motion of the plaintiff for that the defen-
    dant hath not fullfilled the Law in his appeale,
    the Worshippfull Court orders Judgment to bee en-
    tred against the defendant according to the ver-
    dict of the Jury.

John Janson Veryne,[193] Plaintiff
Timotheus Gabriell,[194] Defendant
    The Plaintiff declared that by the unjust and vex-
    atious trickes of the defendant in the tyme of the
    Dutch government hee is damnified to the summe of
           . The Worshippfull Court having heard what
    both parties cold alleadge and the Papers read on

boath sides, the Court Looke upon it as an unjust
molestation and order it to bee soe Entred. The
Court will Consider of the Cost & dammages.

Dirick Smith, Plaintiff
Jacobus Fabricius,[195] defendant
    The Plaintiff declared that the defendant is in
    his debt in the summe of f. 1714 & 17 skeples of
    wheate and hath a Judgment & Execution for the
    same in the tyme of the Dutch Government, where-
    fore prayes a renovation and Confirmation thereof
    with Costs. The worshippfull Court approves of
    and Confirmes the said Judgment, and Orders Exe-
    cution to bee Executed accordingly.

Hump. Davenport, Plaintiff
Gerrit Hugo, Defendant
    The Plaintiff declared for f. 159 for Taffety,
    and the defendant brought his account for the
    summe of £ 04.10 for Phisick to the plaintiff's
    wife. The worshippfull Court orders the defen-
    dant to pay the plaintiff f. 100 and the f. 59 to
    be discounted for Phisick, and each to pay their
    owne Cost.

Jacques Cousow, Plaintiff
Fred. Phillips, Defendant
    The plaintiff desyres that hee may have an account
    of his 7/16 of his shipp the Hopewell; the Court
    desyre Mr. Phillipps to give the plaintiff an ac-
    count thereof against next Court.

Abraham Pierson[196] cum assotiates, Plaintiffs
Nicolaus Bayard, defendant
    The Court finding that Mr. Bayard was not lerned
    with his summons in due tyme, doe order that the
    plaintiff take out a New Summons.

Capt. Antony Billopp, Plaintiff
Tobias Elliston, Defendant
    The Plaintiff declared in an account of defamation.
    The Court finding the defandant wholy uncapable
    of making satisfaction as the Law may require,
    doe order him before the Court to make his humble
    acknowledgment of the wrong done to the plaintiff
    and goe to the plaintiff's wife and on his knees
    to begg her pardon and the same to be recorded.

Mr. Frederick Phillipps, Plaintiff
John Arnold,[197] Defendant
    The plaintiff declared that the defendant is in-
    debted unto him f. 757.14 besides the Charge of
    fetching him back being fledd into New England.
    The Court finding the defendant in many fallacies

& falsehoods doe order him to bee recommitted.

Widdow Harrison's 2 daughters brought in a Petition
which the Court read and ordered that when their
Mother pay her Charges her goods shall be restored
to her againe.

Magdeline Cowenhoven's[198] Petition being read, the
Court doe Order to take a view of the Land in and
about the Citty and to Consider thereof.

John Evertson Karsboome's[199] Petition read for a Carman Place, and order if a vacancy then the petitioner to bee admitted.

Joseph Yates's[200] Petition read for a Porter's place,
the Court the petitioner's admition if a vacancye.

At a Court meeting held in New Yorke on Munday the
26th Aprill 1675.
Present: Mr. Mayor; Mr. Deputy; Mr. Minviele; Mr.
Phillipps.
Matthew Force[201] & Joseph Yates had their Oathes
sworne Porters.

His honnour the Governour sent his order to the Court
to nominate the officers for 3 Companies of Trayne bands
in this Citty, 2 for Each office, which they did as vizt:
Mr. John Winder, C. William Dyre, Mr. Minviele, C. Tho.
Smith, M. De Mayor, C. Salisbury, Mr. Hoghland, Lt. Rum-
bouts, Mr. Gibbs, Step. Cortland, Mr. Van Cleyfe, Mr.
Hans, Mr. Lockerman, Jos. Lawrence, Mr. William Nicolls,
Mr. P. Richards, C. Davenport, Mr. Rugg, Mr. Blagg, Mr.
Jo. Darvall, if they intend to Continue here.

The Worshippfull Mayor and Aldermen went about the
Citty and surveyed all the vacancies of ground and ould
decayed houses as alsoe to finde a Propper place for a
Church and shoemakers Tann Pitts and tooke an account
thereof as in a Paper tytled, the Surveigh of the Citty.

At a Speciall Court held in New Yorke Primo May 1675.
C. Anthony Brockhurst,[202] Plaintiff
Allex. Wardrupp, administrator of
    Samuell Laine,[203] Deceased, Defendant
The plaintiff declared that the defendant was indebted to him before his death the summe of £34
Sterling; the administrator owned that hee heard
the defendant confesse the debt before hee came
out of England. The Court orders Judgment that
the Administrator pay the said debt if soe much
assetts in his hands.

Thomas Ashton, Plaintiff
Samuell Willson, Defendant
> The Plaintiff complained that the defendant will
> not performe the Judgment of Court and moved for
> Execution, whereupon the Court doe order that if
> the defendant doe not pay it speedely Execution
> shall bee issued forth.

The sherriff brought in an account from the Governour of divers Vintners of this Citty in arreare for the Great Excize and demands Execution for the same, which the Court orders accordingly.

Robert Morley, Robert Barret & John Goodacre, being Committed to the Goale of this Citty on suspition of taking away a Calfe from one Steentie Lowrence,[204] Proclamation was made 3 tymes for any accusers to come in, which none appeared, wherefore the Court after sundry admonitions accquitted the Prisoners by proclamation.

John Arnold, a prisoner, being brought to the barr, his petition was taken into Consideration, and the Creditors brought in, whereupon the court ordered hee should bee returned againe to prison till farther order.

Thomas Lovelace, Plaintiff
Cornelius Post, Luycas Tienhoven,
    Samuell Rescoe, Defendants
> The Plaintiff moved for Execution against each of
> these defendants according to former Judgments,
> whereupon the Court ordered them to bee issued
> forth accordingly.

Humphry Davenport, Plaintiff
Gerrit Hugo, Defendant
> The Plaintiff moved for Execution against the de-
> fendant upon a Judgment formerly passed against
> him, which the Court ordered accordingly.

John Sharpe Complaining that the wife[205] of Walter Carr,[206] Taylor in this Citty, deteyned a Laced whiske[207] which was his wife's, it being found in their house, the Sherriff brought it into the Court by order, where after Examination into the matter it appeared by sufficient proofe to belong to the said Sharpe's wife and was not Sold at the Outcry amongst his Lining whereby it was imagined to bee stolen. The Court Order it bee delivered to the Complainant and hee to keepe the same, unless it bee proved it was bought at the outcry.

At a Court meeting held the 9th day of May 1675.
Present: Mr. John Lawrence, Deputy Mayor; Mr. John Winder, Alderman.
Robert Story,[208] Merchant

William Allen,[209] Shoemaker
George Masters,[210] Taylor
Hen. Willis,[211] Carpenter
William Leeds, Cooper
Fran. Cooley, Labourer
    These presented themselves to the Court & request-
ed to bee admitted into the Burgery of this Citty to
the end that they may follow their trade & calling,
which was granted them accordingly Provided they behave
themselves Civilly and pay such accknowledgements as
hereafter shall bee ordered for Strangers admition to
the freedome of this Citty, which they Engaged to doe
when thereunto required.
    This day was Published the Proclamation Prohibiting
the selling any strong liquors to the Indians on the
penalty in the Law sett forth.

    At a Speciall Court held in New Yorke the 27th day of
May In the 27th yeare of his Majestie's Reigne Annoque
Somini 1675.
    Present: C. Mathias Nicolls, Mayor; Mr. John Law-
rence, Deputy; Mr. Gabriell Minviele, Mr. John Winder,
Aldermen.
    Joseph Townesend,[212] Plaintiff
    John Foxall, Defendant
        The Plaintiff's Attorney George Cooke read the de-
        claration which was for £337.14.5 As per account
        produced, attested on Oath by the Plaintiff bee-
        fore Governour Leverets, which was Certefied under
        the hand of the said Governour, with the seale of
        the Messathusets Collony thereunto; divers papers
        produced by the plaintiff & defendant and read in
        Court with the allegations of both parties maturly
        heard and debated, which done the Mayor gave the
        Charge to the Jury of 12 men, who went out and
        after deliberate debate Brought in their Verdict
        as followeth, vizt: The Jury find for the plain-
        tiff that the defendant ought to bee accountable
        to the Plaintiff for the severall parcells of
        goods, ammounting to £337.14.5, which appeares by
        the Plaintiff's account to have bine delivered to
        the defendant and that hee forthwith give security
        for his soe doeing, with Costs of Court.
        The Worshippfull Court accepted the Verdict of the
        Jury And ordered that Judgment bee entred against
        the defendant that hee speedely put in security to
        bee accountable to the plaintiff or his order for
        the said goods delivered in Virginia by the 20th
        day of October next & that hee pay the Costs of
        the Suite.

    This day Mr. John Foxall made oath to what was Ex-
amined him by the Court as in the Court day booke of
this date appears.

At a Court held in New Yorke Primo June 1675.
Present: Mr. Mathias Nicolls, Mayor; Mr. John Law-
rence, Deputy; Mr. Fred Phillipps, Mr. John Winder,
Aldermen.
Arient Isackson, Plaintiff
Wessell Wessells, Defendant
Wessell Wessells, Plaintiff
Arient Isackson, Defendant
 The worshippfull Court having maturly heard what
 both parties could alleage and the witnesses
 sworne the President sent out the Jury with the
 Charge, who after deliberate debate on the matter
 brought in their verdict that they find the acction on boath sides needless and vexatious and
 that each pay ½ the Charge. The worshippfull
 Court thereupon Orderd Judgment to bee entred accordingly, that Plaintiff & Defendant doe Each
 pay the charge of a Jury and that the matter bee
 noe more brought into Court.

Emanuell Mandevile, Plaintiff
Nicolas De Mayor, Defendant
 The defendant's attorney moved for an Appeale to
 the Assizes which the Court allowed.

Ditto, Plaintiff
John Shackerley, Defendant
 The Plaintiff moved for Judgment, which the Court
 order to bee entred according to the Jureys for
 noe verdict.

John Weekes, Plaintiff
John Smeedes, Defendant
 The Court orders Judgment to bee Entred against
 the defendant with Costs.

Isack Molyne,[213] Plaintiff
Dirrick Woolspiner,[214] Defendant
 The Plaintiff declared for 220 lbs. sugar &
 £ 00.17.8. The Court ordered if not good reason
 to the contrary next court Judgment shall be
 Entred against the defendant.

Sarah de Foreest,[215] Plaintiff
Thomas Verdon,[216] Defendant
 The plaintiff declared for money due for an
 Erve[217] sold to the defendant. The Court having
 heard what both parties could alleadge, ordered
 Judgment against the defendant with costs, and the
 plaintiff to give security and good assurance for
 the Land shee sold.

Sarah Hayes, Plaintiff
Josiah Hallet,[218]
    The Plaintiff demanding f. 79, the defendant did
    alleage hee paid the same to the Defendant's
    [sic!] husband but cold not prove the same, where-
    fore the Court ordered Judgment against the defen-
    dant with Costs.

Sarah De Vorreest, Plaintiff
Jan Arianson & Derick Smith, Defendants
    The Court having maturly heard what all persons
    cold alleage, gave the charge to the Jury who
    brought in their verdict for the defendants for
    that they having peaceably & quietly enjoyed the
    said house severall yeares without any molesta-
    tion, according to the Law of this Government and
    that the plaintiff pay costs of Court, The Wor-
    shippfull Court order Judgment to be entred
    accordingly.

    This day by order of the Court a warrant was issued
forth to Mr. Joannes De Pyster, Stephen Van Courtland,
Bolley Rollophson[219] and William White to bee overseers
for the cleansing the great Graft or Ditch, and that
they present the names of the persons who neglect to
doe their parts thereof to the end they may bee fined
for their remissness and contempt, according to law.

    At a Court meeting held in New Yorke the 5th June in
the 27th Yeare of his Majestie's reigne, 1675.
    Present: C. Mathias Nicolls, Mayor; Mr. John Law-
rence, Deputy; Mr. Fred. Phillipps, Alderman.

Proclamation about freedomes of this Citty
    The Court having taken into their Consideracon the
great inconveniencye of Strangers who come heere and
openly sell and retayle their goods, wares and Mer-
chantdizes and exercize their trades and handecrafts
without takeing notice of the Corporation or obteyning
the Priviledge or freedome of this Citty according to
former Order and Custome as well heere as in other
places, Whereupon they thought fitt to order That all
persons whatsoever that live in this Citty or that come
from other parts to trade or Exercise theire Profession,
Function or trade and have not taken out their Burger-
ship or Freedome Shall within Fourteene dayes after the
Publication hereof come and adress themselves to the
Court, the Mayor or his Deputy, who upon Civill be-
haviour and Paying what is hereafter mentioned may be
admitted Accordingly, vizt. The Merchant or Shopkeepers
who deale in Considerable Estate by sea and Land are to
pay Six Beavers or the Equivelent value; the Litle Burger who sell by retayle or exercize their trades, handy-
crafts & professions are to pay Two Beavers on the

penalty of double the value for their default, and
after their admition they are to take out a Certificate
of their Privilledge from the Towne Clearke, who is to
deliver it with the Seale of the Citty fixed thereunto.
Published at the Citty hall the day and yeare above-
written. By John Sharpe, Towne Clearke.

   The Bridges of this Citty being viewed and found
much out of repayre and decayed, and that they Are very
chargable to bee maintained and kept in good Repayre
for the Conveniencye of Strangers Landing their Goods
as well as for use of the Inhabitants of this Gouvern-
ment.
   Wherefore the Court have thought fitt to Order that
all goods whatsoever that shall from henceforth bee
brought into this Government and Landed on the Bridge,
They belonging to Strangers, shall pay Eight pence per
Tunn and Soe proportionable for Lesser quantities, the
freemen or Burgers of this Citty Six pence per tunn and
that in silver or the Equivalent value thereof, Goods
brought from New Jersey and Salt Only Excepted.
   And all Barkes, Ketches, Sloopes or other vessells
with Decks that are fastned to Lye or Leane on the long
Bridge or within the Camber or haven on the West side
thereof after 24 howers Shall pay for each day and
night they shall there continue 2s. silver or its value.
   And other smaller Vessells and open boates without
Deckes One shilling.
   All Sloopes or other Vessells with Deckes that Lye
in the haven or Camber for shelter and security in the
Winter Shall pay One Beaver, and Open Vessells or Boates
the halfe.
   Published at the Citty Hall the day above Written By
John Sharpe, Towne Clearke.
June 22d. 1675

   Tunis Cray, Plaintiff
   Allard Anthony, Defendant
      The Plaintiff declared for f. 626 for dyeting
      Prisoners due by a Judgment long since passed for
      the same. The Worshippfull Court have heard what
      both parties Cold alleadge. Ordered Judgment
      againe to bee entred against the defendant for
      f. 322 & the f. 118 the other post of f. 184 if
      the defendant prove not the Same or part thereof
      paid, then to pay it or the remainder & all Costs.

   Allexander Bryan,[220] Plaintiff
   Elizab. Bedloo, Defendant
      The Plaintiff declared for £129:09:06; the Court
      having heard what both parties cold say, their
      Evidences sworne, gave the charge to the Jury, who
      brought in their verdict for the plaintiff with
      Costs. The Court order Judgment to bee entred

accordingly. The defendant moved for Appeale,
which was granted.

Lowr. Vander Spiegle, Plaintiff
Elizab. Bedloo, Defendant
    The plaintiff declared for f. 4212:13. The wor-
    shippfull Court heard what was to bee alleaged on
    both sides and gave the charge to the Jury, who
    Brought in their verdict for the Plaintiff. The
    worshippfull Court ordered Judgment to bee entred
    against the defendant with Costs. The defendant
    moved for an appeale, which was granted.

Elias Doughty, Plaintiff
Eliz. Bedloo, Defendant
    The Plaintiff declared for £27 for 4 Oxen sold and
    delivered to her husband in his life tyme. The
    Jury brought in their verdict for the Plaintiff
    And the worshippfull Court Ordered Judgment to bee
    Entred accordingly. An appeale being desyred was
    granted accordingly.

Luycas Tienhoven, Plaintiff
Pieter Paulus,[221] Defendant
    The Plaintiff declared for f. 125 for 5 years
    trimming. The matter being maturly heard, the
    Court ordered Judgment against the defendant with
    Costs.

Isack Molyne, Plaintiff
Michaell Smith,[222] defendant
    The Plaintiff declared for £14.5.11¼ Due for
    freight. Both parties with their proofes being
    deliberately heard, the Worshippfull Court Order
    Judgment against the plaintiff for that it
    appeares to bee unjust molestation and condemn
    him to pay costs.

James Bullin,[223] Plaintiff
Tho. Taylor, Defendant
    The Plaintiff declared for £2.10.0 of the defen-
    dant. The defendant not appearing but being the
    second default, the Court order Judgment against
    him with Costs.

Mr. Michaell Smith produceing authentique power from
John Barrey of Barbados, the nearest relation of C.
Thomas Badgard[224] deceased, moved to bee admitted Sub-
administrator to the said Badgard's Estate, which the
Court granted accordingly, Provided hee act according a
in the lawes of this government is prescribed and put i
security for his performing and fullfilling thereof.

At an additionall Court held the 24 June 1675.
Present: Mr. Mayor; Mr. Deputy; Mr. Phillipps,
Mr. Minviele, Mr. Winder, Aldermen.
Capt. William Dyre, Plainyiff
Egidius Luyke, Defendant
    The plaintiff as attorney for his R. Highness de-
    clared for f. 317.15.8 in Beavers & f. 6319.15
    seawant by bonds due to Collonell Lovlace, which
    were owned by the defendant before the Court,
    whereupon the Jury went out with their Charge and
    brought in their verdict for the Plaintiff that
    the defendant forthwith pay f. 8541 seawant or by
    Value equivalent, finding soe much due to the Bal-
    lance of accounts with Costs of suite. The
    Court orders Judgment to bee entred accordingly.
    Upon the motion of the plaintiff for Execution &
    the defendant for a review, the court order Exe-
    cution to bee issued forth & if the defendant
    hath any Lawfull Exception to any part of the
    account in which hee pretends a mistake, the same
    being alsoe intimated by some other persons to
    the court, hee may address him to Equity for re-
    leife therein.

30 ditto. Execution   primo August following.

At an Additionall Court 24 June 1675
The Bench Compleat.

Mr. Thomas Gibbs, Mr. John Sharpe, Mr. Hen. Newton,
Complaining they cannot gett their fees, upon which the
Worshippfull Court doe Order if persons doe not pay
their fees by civill and fayre demands, the Sherriff
hath power to Leavy the same by distress or Execution.

    Frederick Phillipps, Plaintiff
    Jaques Coussow, Defendant
    The Declaration and answer being read, the Court
    finding it matter of account & great difficulty
    therein, doe request Mr. Joannes De Piester, Mr.
    Rumbout, Mr. Steenwyck, Mr. Stephanus Van Cortland
    to peruse the accounts and to bring the same into
    as briefe a method for the finding out the differ-
    rence as possible they can and make a report there-
    of to the next Court.

The Court doe recommend the Care of surveying and
cleansing the great Ditch or graft of this Citty unto
Mr. Joannes De Piester, Stephanus Van Cortland and William White, and they are desyred to see the same per-
fected.

Nicolas Bayard, Plaintiff
John Rider, Defendant
    The Papers being read and what could bee alleadg-
    ed on boath sides, the Jury went out and brought
    in their verdict for the Plaintiff that the de-
    fendant pay him f. 1800.4 in Seawant or goods
    equivelent, with interest for the same, and that
    the Defendant pay Costs. The Court order Judgment
    to bee entred accordingly.

Hugo Barnson, Plaintiff
Daniell De Haert, Defendant
    The Court haveing heard what Could bee alleaged
    on bothe sides, the Jury went out and brought in
    their verdict for the defendant with Cost. The
    Court orders Judgment to bee entred accordingly.

At a Spetiall Court held June the 30th 1675.
Present: Mr. Mayor; Mr. Deputy; Mr. Winder.

William Foresight, Plaintiff
Richard Hall,[225] Defendant
    The worshippfull Court having heard what both
    parties could alleadge sent out the Jury, Who
    brought in their verdict for the Plaintiff that
    the defendant shall pay what wages is due to the
    Plaintiff with Costs. The Court order Judgment
    to bee entred accordingly But to be paid out of
    the owner's effects or goods.

At a Court held the 27 July 1675.
Present: Mr. Mayor; Mr. Deputy; Mr. Minviele.

Josia Johnson, Plaintiff
Nath. Spratt, Defendant
    The plaintiff brought in a warrant of Attorney to
    Mr. Cooke or Mr. West to confesse a Judgment for
    £11.12, which the Court order to bee entred but
    suspend Execution till further order.

William Radney,[226] Jos. Lee,[227] Prosecutors
    for the King, Plaintiffs
Peter Gerritz,[228] Defendant
    The Plaintiffs declared that the defendant's
    Ketch and Cargoe belonged to Dutch owners and
    manned with Dutchmen contrary to act of parliment
    to trade in this Port, etc. The Court having ex-
    amined all the testimonies and read the papers,
    the Jury gave in their verdict for the Plaintiffs
    and finde the Ketch with her Cargoe imported & Ex
    ported are forfeited by the act of trade and Navi
    gation. The Court received the verdict and order
    Judgment to bee entred accordingly. The defendan
    moved for an appealle but Lett it fall.

Hen. Brazier,[229] Plaintiff
Richard Hall, Defendant
   The Court haveing heard what both partyes could
   alleadge ordered C. Davenport, the defendant's
   attorney, to pay the plaintiff 40s. and the defendant to pay Costs.

Mr. Gabriell Minviele, Plaintiff
Joannes Smedes, Defendant
   The Plaintiff declared that the defendant deteyn-
   ed 18 Sackes which cost him 18 guilders each. The
   Court order the defendant to returne the sackes
   or make payment for them and pay Costs.

John Carman,[230] Plaintiff
Arian Laer,[231] Defendant
   The Plaintiff declared that the defendant owed
   him 31 Bushell of winter wheate. The Court order
   Judgment if not reason to the contrary next Court.

Abell Hardenbrooke, Plaintiff
Thom. Taylor, Defendant
   The Plaintiff declared for f. 81 wampom value.
   The court order the defendant to agree with the
   Plaintiff, otherwise to grant Judgment against
   the defendant with Costs.

William Radney, Plaintiff
.... Fulker, Defendant
   The Court desyred the plaintiff to pass by the af-
   front and the defendant to pay Costs.

John Janson, Plaintiff
Timoth. Gabry, Defendant
   The Court order that this Case bee by them taken
   into consideration betweene this and the next
   Court day.

Nath. Spratt, Plaintiff
Tho. Taylor, Defendant
   The Court ordered Judgment against the defendant
   to pay the remainder with Costs of suite.

Abell Hardenbrooke, Plaintiff
Elias Provost,[232] Defendant
   The plaintiff declared for f. 164 wampom. The
   Court order the sherriff to nominate 2 persons
   and they to pay the charge if they agree not.

The Court adjourned untill Saturday 31.

At a Court held in New Yorke July 31 1675.
   Present: Mr. Mayor; Mr. Deputy; Mr. Darvall; Mr.
Phillipps; Mr. Minviele.

Robert Bowman, Latly of Southhold, was brought to
this Court and indighted for feloniously stealing certaine Lining, a molotto slave and a Canew from Mr.
Michaell Smith, etc. Hee pleaded Guilty in Generall.
Upon deliberate debate on the matter of the malifactor,
the Court doe order and pass sentence that the malefac-
tor shall receive 39 stripes at the whipping post before the Citty Hall on Munday next at 11 of the Clocke
in the forenoone and afterwards bee returned to his
Master John Budd[233] to whome hee shall give an indentur
for 5 yeares service in consideration of the charge &
dammage and 6 months more in consideration of the Losse
& dammage Mr. Michaell Smith hath susteyned. The Execution was done accordingly.

John Shackerley, Plaintiff
Emanuell Mandevile, Defendant
    Upon the motion of the Plaintiff about the Negro
    hee bought (of the defendant) the Court in Consid
    eration of his Loss doe finde it convenient that
    Mr. Mandevile doe pay the costs of suite and doe
    order it accordingly.

Andrew Ball,[234] brought out of Prison to the Barr,
being indighted for taking a false Oath before the
Governour to defraud his Majestie of his right, as well
as to obstruct due Course of Justice, etc. The Prisone
Pleaded Guilty to the Indightment and begged the mercy
of the Court, Upon whose petitione and being a Long tym
in Prison, the worshippfull Court doe sentence that the
said Andrew Ball bee on Munday next brought to the whip
ping post before the Citty Hall and there continue
standing with a Paper pinned on his breast mention his
Crime for the Space of One whole hower.

Capt. William Dyre Petitioned the Court for a writt
of Appraisment of the Ketch Suzanna and her goods Im-
ported and Exported. The Court doe grant it and doe
appoynt and desyre Capt. Nath. Davenport, Capt. Tho.
Smith, Mr. Francis Smith, Mr. Tho. Lewis and Mr. Willia
Woodgate to be appraisers.

Allexander Bryan, Plaintiff
Elizabeth Bedloo, Defendant
    Capt. Davenport, the Plaintiff's Attorney, moved
    the Court for Execution on the former Judgment,
    shee having not put in security to prosecute her
    appeale according to Law. The Court order it to
    bee done by the midle of the next weeke.

John Rider moved the Court that the will of Mr. Roge
Rugg might be recorded, which was ordered & was as
followeth: Wee who have hereunto Subscribed doe declar
and are ready to testifye that on Saturday the 24 July

last Mr. Roger Rugg, being taken very sick and fearing
his death, did in our hearing answer to his honnour the
Governour Severall questions, amongst the rest that hee
hoped hee had made his peace with God for his eternall
happiness, and, being asked by his honnour how hee
would dispose of his worldly affayres, hee answered
that hee Left all hee had to Mr. Rider and his wife,
they paying his debts. His honnour, desyring to know
if any more should bee concerned then Mr. Rider, hee
answered that hee desyred Capt. Davenport to assist him
but gave all that hee had to Mr. Rider and his wife and
told her hee had given all hee had to her & her husband,
saying I give you my negro Boy Mingo to yourselfe; bee
kinde to him for my sake. The said Mr. Rugg upon the
29th July did severall tymes declare to us that the will
hee had made Publiquly before the Governour and others
should stand good, that Mr. Rider and his wife should
have all hee had in the world, and farther wee testifye
that hee was very sensible both dayes when hee declared
this his will unto us, in testimony whereof wee sub-
scribe the 30th July 1675: Hartman Wessells, John
Jourdaine, Tho. Coker,[235] Hen. Clearke,[236] John Col-
lier.[237]

At a Court meeting held in New Yorke the 2d. of
August 1675.

John Rider moveing the Court that the goods and
effects of Mr. Roger Rugg might bee inventaried, there
being some that were in a decaying and perishing condition, the Court, finding very meete and requisite, doe
desyre & appoynt C. Nathaniell Davenport, Mr. Thomas
Gibbs and Mr. John Sharpe to view, surveigh & Inventary
the same and to doe it with what Expedition may bee,
which was done accordingly the next day.

At a Court meeting held the 7th August 1675.

Mrs. Elizabeth Bedloo, having Petitioned his honnour
the Governour to bee admitted Administratrix to her
late deceased husband and to have the bookes and accounts to the end that shee might receive and make
Payment of the debts, etc., upon which his honnour re-
commended the said matter to bee considered of and by
the Mayor and aldermen of this Citty, who are to make
their report and Oppinion therein to his honnour as
soone as possible. The which was ordered accordingly
and the report thereof made to his honnour and shee had
her bookes and Papers delivered to her and an Inventary
thereof taken by mee the Clearke in presents of Capt.
Nicolls.

John Rider, administrator to Mr. Roger Rugg deceased,
informed the Court that his honnour the Governour

referred the business of Mr. Roger Rugg's Estate to
this Court, whose oppinion was that Mr. Rider put in
security for the discharge of his administratorship to
the summe of £500 Sterling and that the goods with all
other things belonging to the said Mr. Roger Rugg bee
Inventaried before Mr. Rider receive the Same, and that
hee shall have accustomary Commission for the sales of
the goods and to give an account thereof with all other
the said Estate when thereunto required.

In order thereunto Mr. William Darvall, Mr. Thomas
Gibbs & Mr. John Sharpe are desyred to take an account
and inventarize the Goods, Papers, Bookes, bills, bonds
& other things of the said Roger Rugg and to deliver to
John Rider the f. 1000 wampom and 53 Beavers to defray
Funerall Charges and other contingent expenses and
Charges relating to the said estate.

At a Mayor's Court held in New Yorke the 17th August
1675.

John Carman, Plaintiff
Arian Van Laer, Defendant
    The Plaintiff declared for 31 Bushell of winter
    wheate due to him by bill. The Court, haveing
    heard what both could alleadge, Ordered Judgment
    against the Defendant for what is remayning due
    to the plaintiff with Costs, but suspend Execution
    till farther Order.

Mr. Gabriell Minviele, Plaintiff
Cornelis Van Bursen,[238] Defendant
    The Court finding the debt due and the defendant
    not appearing, doe order Judgment against him,
    with Costs.

Ditto, Plaintiff
Henry Vandewater,[239] Defendant
    The plaintiff having proved his debt and the de-
    fendant having made 3 defaults, the Court order
    Judgment with Costs.

Ditto, Plaintiff
Jan Van Bomell[240] & Peter Peterson,[241] Defendants
    The Court order the Plaintiff give the defendants
    Credit for what hee hath received and Judgment for
    the rest due with Costs.

Nehemiah Pierce, Plaintiff
Dirrick Smith, Defendant
    The Plaintiff demanded £22.17 Boston silver & 35
    lb. of Beaver. The defendant pretending hee hath
    paid part thereof, the Court Order Judgment if not
    composed by next Court.

James Mathewes, Plaintiff
Nicolaus Bayard, Defendant
  In this Case the Court doe desyre Mr. William
  Croadsby, Mr. Jac. Vandewater[242] and Mr. William
  Darvall to bee present to view the Bookes of the
  Defendant and make their returne next Court.

Hen. Eason, Plaintiff
John Watkins,[243] Defendant
John Watkins, Plaintiff
Eliz Ferne & Uxor, Defendant - Crosse Action
  The Court haveing maturely heard what both
  parties could alleadge sent out the Jury, who
  after a long debate brought in their verdict for
  the defendant and the plaintiff to pay Costs. The
  Court accept of the verdict of the Jury and order
  Judgment to bee Entred accordingly.

Mathew Force, Plaintiff
John Watkins, Defendant   In an acction of Defama-
                             tion.
  Both parties being heard, the president Gave the
  Charge to the Jury, who went out and brought in
  their verdict for the Plaintiff with Costs. The
  Court accept of the verdict and order Judgment to
  bee entred against the defendant accordingly.

Paulus Richard,[244] Plaintiff
Nicolas Manera, Defendant
  The Plaintiff declared for f. 258.2 wampon. The
  defendant confessing the debt, the Court order
  Judgment to bee entred against him, that hee pay
  the plaintiff in the Spring what is justly due
  with Costs.

Joannes Verveile,[245] Plaintiff
John Archer, Defendant
  The Plaintiff declared for a Parcell of hay Cut
  off his meadowes. The Court orders the Plaintiff
  to have his Lease and the defendant to have his
  payment and desyre Mr. Gibbs and Mr. Webly to surveigh the meadow and to make their report, who
  after surveigh brought it in, which was Vizt.,
  that the meadow in Controversye belonged to the
  Plaintiff, the defendant to pay Costs.

John Sharpe, Plaintiff
John Rider, Defendant
  Upon the Plaintiff's motion for Execution against
  the defendant upon the Judgment passed 8th March
  Last, the Worshippfull Court doe order the Clearke
  to issue it out accordingly and to signe the same
  in the name of the court.

Abell Hardenbrooke, Plaintiff
Elias Provost, Defendant
   The arbiters having brought in their report,
   therby the Court find that the money or rent demanded by the Plaintiff not due by reason the
   house is not tenantable and order the plaintiff
   to pay Costs.

Jacobus De Haert brought in 2 Executions, the one
against Abell Hardenbrooke, the other against Peter Janson Van Werkendam,[246] and desyred they might bee Confirmed and Executed. The Court order if they shew not
reason the next Court to the Contrary it shall proceed
accordingly.

James Mathewes, Plaintiff
Nicolas Bayard, Defendant
   The Plaintiff declared for f. 500 wampoms value.
   The Court finds the Plaintiff's debt due from the
   Citty, which the Court conceive ought to bee paid,
   but the Plaintiff to pay Cost of suite.

Nicolas Bayard, Plaintiff
James Mathewes, Defendant
   The Court haveing heard what both parties could
   alleadge, doe conclude that Mr. Bayard ought to
   have the vendue money of the defendant and order
   Judgment with Costs but noe Execution till further
   order.

Abell Hardenbrooke, Plaintiff
Elias Provost, Defendant
   The Plaintiff making it appeare that the former
   arbitrators were the neare relations of the defendant and of his owne Choosing, not according to
   the order of this Court, the Court are pleased to
   appoynt Mr. Adolph[247] and Jeremias, Carpinters,
   to surveigh the said house and bring in their report next Court.

Mr. Gabriell Minviele moves for Executions against
Jan Van Bomell & Peter Peterson, Hendrick Vande Water,
Jan Smedes, Corn. Van Bursen. The Court order that the
Clearke doe issue them forth accordingly.

Nicolas Bayard Petitioned the Court to Explaine the
Judgment of Court past against John Rider on the 24th
June last, in answer to which the Court doe finde that
Mr. Rider must pay the rest of the vendue money in
Spetie according to the conditions of the vendue, as was
then and therein Exprest, & as it appeares the house did
and doth belong to John Rider, so the Charges must con-
sequently follow to Nicolas Bayard for the last sale or
vendue.

Paulus Richards, Plaintiff
Nicolas Manera, Defendant
    Upon the Petition of Paulus Richards the Court
    order that the defendant put in Sufficient Secu-
    rity for his performance of the former Judgment
    of the Court, otherwise Execution to bee issued
    against him for the same.

John Sharpe, Plaintiff
William White,[248] Defendant
    The Court order both Parties to draw up their Ex-
    ceptions against each others accounts in writting
    and desyre Mr. Jacob Vandewater and Mr. Ephraim
    Harmanson[249] to Examine and view the said ac-
    counts and to make their report to the next Court.

At a Court held   September 1675.
The Court Compleate.

Robert Leprerye,[250] Plaintiff
Jacob Molynes,[251] Defendant
    The Declaration & plea on both sides being read
    and all the wittnesses heard & Examined, the Jury
    went out and brought in their verdict for the
    Plaintiff that the defendant pay unto him £150
    Sterling for Expence and dammage with Costs. The
    Court Orders Judgment to bee Entred accordingly.
    The Defendant moved the Court to grant him a re-
    view, which was granted him Provided hee Performe
    what the law requires in such Cases.

    Courateurs of Balthazar De Haert move the Court for
their sallary and Expences about the said Estate and
for a discharge from their said trust and Confirmation
of the award of the good men. The court replyed they
would consider thereof and that the administrators shall
have the bookes & Papers delivered to them upon giveing
an accquittance for what they receive. The court desyre
Mr. Darvall to bee present when they are delivered.

Cornelius Clopper,[252] Plaintiff
Nicolas Bayard, Defendant
    The Plaintiff demands f. 1706.19, & the court or-
    ders that if the defendant doe not pay it in 2
    moneths then the plaintiff to have Judgment for
    the said debt with Cost against the defendant.

William Radney Moved the Court for Judgment for the
1/3 part of the Beavers, etc., seized on board the Burss.
of Amsterdam. The Court Orders Judgment accordingly.

William Pattison[253] by his Attorneys, Plaintiff
Jacob Vandewater, Defendant
    They declared that the defendant obteyned a

Certaine house and Land in this Citty belonging
to the said William Pattison. The Court haveing
maturely heard what could bee alleadged on boath
sides Gave the Jury the charge, who went out and
brought in their verdict that they find for the
Plaintiff that the defendant give the plaintiff
possession of the said house and premisses with
Cost of suite.

William Pattison, Plaintiff
Lodowyck Post,[254] Dirick Evertson Floyd,[255] Peter
    Harmanson,[256] defendants
The Plaintiff declared against each of the defendants that they each of them deteyned a certaine
house and accomodations, etc. from the said plaintiff. The Jury brought in their verdict as in
the case of Jacob Vandewater as above. Thereupon
the Court order Judgment to bee Entred against
them all foure with Costs. They all moved for
appeale, which was granted them.

Elizabeth Bedloo, Plaintiff
Cornelis Van Bursen, Defendant
The Plaintiff declared that the defendant had
effects of Mr. Cornelius Van Ruyvens[257] in his
hands, who was in her debt f. 161 wampom, as per
bill. The Court order Judgment for the plaintiff
with Costs, but the Plaintiff to put in security
to repay it if it appeares not due.

Phillip Udall,[258] Plaintiff
John Rider, John Luidley,[259] Defendants
The Plaintiff desyres Judgment against the defen-
dants for 2000 lbs. Tobaccoe due by bond. The
Court orders Judgment against the defendants with
Costs.

Mr. William Darvall, Plaintiff
Egidius Luyke, Defendant
The Plaintiff declared for sundry goods, etc., according to declaration. Both parties being heard,
they gave the charge to the Jury, who brought in
their verdict for the Plaintiff with Costs. The
defendant moved for an appeale to the Court of
Assizes, which was granted.

Ralph Hutchinson,[260] Plaintiff
Tho. Taylor, Defendant
The Plaintiff's declaration being read and the
defendant not appearing in 3 Courts, the Court ordered Judgment to bee entred against the defendant
by default and pay Costs.

Mr. William Darvall, Plaintiff
Thomas Williams, Defendant
   The Plaintiff declared for Cables & Cordidge to
   the value of £25. The defendant owned that hee
   bought the same Cables & rigging of John Shackerley. The Jury went out and brought in their verdict for the plaintiff with Costs. The Court ordered Judgment to bee entred against the defendant
   with Costs.

Mr. William Darvall, Plaintiff
Jacob Van De Watter, Defendant
   The Plaintiff declared for 6 turky worke Chayres,
   cost £10. The Jury went out and brought in their
   verdict for the plaintiff with Costs of suite.
   The Court order Judgment accordingly.

Katherne Purchace,[261] Plaintiff
William Churcher, Defendant
   The Plaintiff declared for f. 104. The Court having heard what both parties could alleadge, doe
   Order Judgment to bee entred against the defendant
   with Costs of suite, but the plaintiff to sweare
   to her whole accounts.

Tho. Wandall, plaintiff
Tho. Walton, Defendant
   The plaintiff declares for 1000 shingles. The
   Court orders the Plaintiff to send for them and
   to pay the defendant for them when received and
   each pay the halfe the Costs of suite.

Nicolas De Mayor, Plaintiff
Anthony De Mellt, Defendant
   The Plaintiff declared for f. 647.5 in Beavers &
   f. 283.18 in wampom. The defendant making default, the Court order the defendant to compose
   the matter against next Court, otherwise Judgment.

Nehemiah Pierce, Plaintiff
Dirrick Smith, Defendant
   The parties on boath sides being heard, the Court
   order Judgment against the defendant with Cost.

Kath Purchase, plaintiff
Hen. Hedger,[262] defendant
   The Plaintiff's declaration being read, the Court
   order the defendant to pay the plaintiff f. 50
   besides the f. 16 due to her, and each to pay the
   cost of the Arbitration, But the defendant to pay
   the ordinary cost of suite.

Thomas Gibbs, Plaintiff
John Archer, Defendant
    The Court desyre Mr. P. Jacobs and Dirrick Van
    Cleife to Examine the matter of accounts, estate
    fees & costs and to make a returne thereof next
    court.

Margaret Stevenson,[263] Plaintiff
Daniell De Haert, Defendant
    The Court desyre Mr. Joannes De Piester, Nicolas
    De Mayor, Gerritt Van Tricht[264] & Gelyne Verplanc
    to view & Examine the account of Plaintiff and
    defendant in order to the stating or bringing the1
    to a narrow Compass for the Court's more facile
    understanding the merritt of the cause and to
    bring in a report thereof next court.

John Sharpe, Plaintiff
William White, Defendant
    The arbitrators brought in their award, which the
    Court accepted of and order Judgment to bee entre
    accordingly with Costs, but the charge of arbi-
    tration to bee divided betweene them.

Martine Mayor Upon complaint of his wife, the Court
orders Mr. Lee to deliver the stonnes againe, otherwise
to pay for them, and Costs.

September 21 1675. The Court Compleat.

Nath. Spratt, Plaintiff
William Sturt, Defendant
    The Plaintiff having attached goods of the defen-
    dant's and hee not appearing to defend or answer
    the said attachment, the Court order Judgment
    against the defendant that hee pay the debt due
    with Cost.

Jacobus De Haert, Plaintiff
Abell Hardenbrooke, Defendant
    The Court demands pay for an ancor of Rumm. The
    Court orders Judgment against the defendant to pa
    what is due with Costs.

John Robinson,[265] Plaintiff
Richard Smith of Smithfeild, Defendant
    The Plaintiff's declaration being read and the
    defendant not appearing in 2 Courts, the worshipp
    full Court ordered Judgment to bee entred against
    the defendant with Costs.

Suert Olphert,[266]Plaintiff
Dan. De Haert, Defendant
    The Plaintiff declared for a remayning summe due

upon account for worke hee hath done for Mr.
Balthazar De Haert. The worshippfull Court Order
the defendant to pay what is due to the plaintiff
with Cost.

John Robinson, Plaintiff
C. Thomas Smith, Defendant
    The plaintiff's declaration being read, the defen-
    dant not appearing, the Court orders Judgment
    against the defendant with Costs.

Tho. Lovelace, Plaintiff
Smith & Haert, defendants
    The Plaintiff declared for £10.8.0 due to him for
    sheepe, etc. One of the defendants Owned the
    debt. The court ordered Judgment against the de-
    fendants with Costs.

Mr. Thomas Gibbs, Plaintiff
William White, Robert Hambleton, Defendants.
    The Plaintiff's declaration being read, the Court
    orders Mr. Hambleton or White to pay the plaintiff
    5½ lb. of hopps that are in Season and merchant-
    able and pay Costs.

        Carman, Plaintiff
Arian Van Laer, Defendant
    The Court haveing heard what could bee alleadged,
    doe order Judgment against the defendant that hee
    pay to the plaintiff what is due to him with Costs
    unless hee can make it appeare Henry Ore hath
    paid for the Ox.

Robert Leprery, Plaintiff
Jacob Molyne, Defendant
    The Plaintiff brought his account of Dammage and
    defamation, £400 Sterling. Both parties and witt-
    nesses being heard, Papers and Evidences being
    read, the president gave the charge to the Jury,
    who brought in their verdict for the Plaintiff as
    in writing.

Mr. Gab. Minviele, Plaintiff
Jacob Molynes, Defendant
    The Plaintiff's declaration was read for f. 980 in
    Beavers. The defendant disownes the charge. The
    court heard what each party could alleage with
    what their witnesses had to say, Gave the Charge
    to the Jury, who went out and brought in their
    verdict for the Plaintiff if the declaration be-
    fore the Publique notary bee allowed for evidence
    by the Court, if not the Jury find for the defen-
    dant.

Otto Gerrittz, Plaintiff
Bart. Wessells, Defendant
  The Plaintiff declared in an acction of defamation, £40 dammage. The Court orders Judgment
  against the plaintiff and this Case to bee turned
  out of Court and pay Costs.

John Sharpe, Plaintiff
Frederick Hoy,[267] Defendant
  The Plaintiff declared for f. 146.10 wampon. The
  defendant making 3 defaults and it appearing hee
  was lawfully summoned, the Court ordered Judgment
  against him with Cost.

Eliz. Bedloo, Plaintiff
Corn. Clopper, Defendant
  The Plaintiff declared for f. 94 wampom. The
  Court order Judgment against the defendant to pay
  the same with Costs.

Cornelis Wynhaert,[268] Plaintiff
Nicolas Bayard, Defendant
  The Plaintiff declared for f. 148.19 seawant. The
  Court order Judgment against the defendant if he
  pay it not before next Court with Costs of suite.

Jacob De Haert, Plaintiff
P. Janson Van Werkendam, Defendant
  The Court order a Confirmation of the former Judg-
  ment, and that the defendant make payment with
  Costs.

Mr. William Darvall, Plaintiff
Martine Mayor, Defendant
  The Plaintiff declared for a house Premisses, etc.
  The Court haveing heard what could been alleadged
  on both sides. The Jury had their Charge, who
  brought in their verdict for the Plaintiff and
  that the defendant give present posession & Pay
  Costs. The Court order Judgment accordingly. The
  defendant moved for appeale, which was granted.

Nicolas Bayard, Plaintiff
John Rider, Defendant
  The Plaintiff complained hee could not gett the
  former Execution Executed. The Court order it be
  duely attended and that it bee Executed accordingly.

Phillip Udoll, by his attorney moved for an Explana-
tion of the former Judgment. The Court order John Rider
to pay 6 per cent in place of the penalty.

The Courateurs of Balthazar De Haert. The Court
orders that the Executors have a Coppy of the report of
the Gentlemen appoynted and to make a finall determina-
tion thereof without delay.

Whereas sundry Complaints have bine made to this
Court that the Executions of the Court are not duely
Executed according to Law or the Intent of the Court by
the Sherriff, Therefore for the Prevention of Complaints of the like nature for the future, the Worshippfull Court doe order that the sherriff shall Execute
all Such writts or Execution as shall bee to him
directed by or before the sitting of the next Court,
after the same shall bee to him directed and delivered.
John Sharpe.

ABBREVIATIONS USED IN THE FOOTNOTES

Burghers = *The Burghers of New Amsterdam and The Freemen of
New York, Collections of the New-York Historical
Society for the Year 1885* (N.Y.: The New-York
Historical Society, 1886).

Dutch Mss. = *Calendar of Dutch Historical Manuscripts in the Office
of the Secretary of State, Albany, New York 1630-
1664* (Albany: Weed, Parsons and Company,
1865).

Eng. Mss. = *Calendar of Historical Manuscripts in the Office of
the Secretary of State, Albany, N.Y., Part II*
(Albany: Weed, Parsons and Company, 1866).

MCC = *Minutes of the Common Council of the City of New York 1675-
1776* (N.Y.: Dodd, Mead & Co., 1905).

RNA = *The Records of New Amsterdam from 1653 to 1774* (Baltimore: Genealogical Publishing Co., Inc., 1976).

Wills = *Abstracts of Wills on File in the Surrogate's Office, City of
New York, Collections of the New-York Historical Society
for the Year 1892* (N.Y.: The New-York Historical
Society, 1893).

NOTES:

[1]William White on 10 Nov. 1676 was taxed for a new dock
and on 24 July 1677 for 2 houses and a workhouse
[MCC 1:34 and 59].

[2]Lot No. 4, adjoining the Lutheran congregation in the
garden, and formerly belonging to the West India Company, was granted to George Cobbett on 22 May 1674
[Eng. Mss. 33:25-433]. His property at the market
place and Broadway was assessed on 24 July 1677
[MCC 1:54].

[3]William Welch in 1692 was doorkeeper and messenger of
the house of representatives [Eng. Mss. 38:102].

[4]Claus Ditloo on 28 Feb. 1667 was reported as having no
chimney in his house [MCC 1:42].

[5]George Walsgrave was elected a constable 14 Sept. 1686
[MCC 1:182].

[6]Roger Purchase, it was stated at a court martial held 7
Dec. 1667 in Fort James, with drawn sword had denied
entrance to quarters of Sgt. Dondell. [Wills 1:80].
In 1671 Purchase was apparently keeping a tavern, for
he sued Henry Hodger on account of debt for meat and
drink [RNA 6:283].

[7]John Watkins was listed as a public carter on 13 Feb.
1671/2 [RNA 6:360]. He was taxed for a new dock on 10
Nov. 1676 [MCC 1:35].

[8]Thomas Griffin on 17 Oct. 1677 was discharged as a
carman for not obeying command and doing his duty
[MCC 1:64]. He was appointed carman again on 5 May
1679 and again discharged on 29 Mar. 1684
[MCC 1:73 & 146].

[9]Sym/Symon/Simonus Lucas, carman, was discharged 17 Oct
1677 for not obeying command and doing his duty but
was re-admitted carman in 1679 [MCC 1:64 & 73]. On
18 Aug. 1673 he had promised to work 2 days gratis for
the city [RNA 6:401].

[10]Peter Wessells was discharged 17 Oct. 1677 for not
obeying command and doing his duty but then was fined
and re-admitted [MCC 1:64 & 65].

[11]William Cooke was taxed for a new dock on 10 Nov. 1676
[MCC 1:34]. On 17 Oct. 1677 he was discharged as a
carman for not obeying command and doing his duty but
was re-appointed 5 May 1679 [MCC 1:64 & 73]. On 24
Apr. 1691 Hermpje (widow of William's son Thomas)
petitioned for letters of administration on the estate
of William Cooke [Eng. Mss. 37:45].

[12]John Depape is mentioned on 1 Mar. 1683/4 as owner of
an open boat in an inquiry concerning dock arrears
[MCC 1:128]. John leased land at Gouanis from Paulus
van der Beek, who sued him in 1661 [The Register of Salo-
mon Lachaire (Baltimore: Genealogical Publishing Co.,
Inc., 1978), p. 67].

[13]Jan Langestraat on 25 Jan. 1669/70 was appointed one o
the two branders of all horses and cattle in Manhattan

and on 1 Mar. 1669/70 was elected one of the three overseers of roads and fences [RNA 6:215 & 222]. On 18 Apr. 1691 and on 15 Oct. of the same year was appointed one of the two captains of the carmen [MCC 1:218 & 345]. On 16 Sept. 1690 he had complain- ed that he was deprived of his share of prizes taken in the Canada expedition [Eng. Mss. 36:108].

[14] A Thomas Moore was a resident of Southold in Sept. 1680 [Eng. Mss. 29:237 & 240].

[15] William Darvall on 2 Dec. 1674 put up a bond for the security of the boat in controversy between him and Peter Alricks of Delaware [Eng. Mss. 24:27].

[16] John Tudor/Tuder was made a freeman of NYC on 24 Nov. 1675 [Burghers 40]. A marriage license was granted him and Mrs. Mary Brett on 9 Sept. 1697 [Wills 1:281].

[17] Capt. Nathaniel Davenport, of Boston, merchant, on 3 July 1672 was admitted to be a burgher of NYC [RNA 6:315].

[18] Rodger Rugg, of NYC, merchant, left his estate to Mr. and Mrs. John Rider. John Rider was appointed admin- istrator on 9 Aug. 1675 [Wills 1:30].

[19] John Tucker helped to take the inventory of the estate of Henry Perrin/Perring, of Brookhaven. On 1 Feb. 1675 letters of administration were granted to Perrin's widow Hannah [Wills 1:33].

[20] John West held the office of City Clerk of NYC [Burghers 53].

[21] Dirrick Van Cleaf's wife was Mrs. Geesie Hendricks, daughter of Hendrick Williams [Wills 1:237].

[22] William Bogardus was a notary public [Wills 1:473].

[23] Jacob Lockerman was the son of Govert Lockerman and Mary Jansen [Wills 1:60-61 and Eng. Mss. 40:93].

[24] Peter De La Noy, brother of Abraham De Lanoy, died before 20 Nov. 1696, when his will was proved. His wife Mary, daughter of Samuel Edsall, was named exe- cutrix [Wills 1:268-269]. In Dec. 1689 Peter had been appointed receiver of the revenues of the pro- vince and in 12 Dec. Mayor of NYC [Eng. Mss. 36:142].

[25] Humphrey Davenport was taxed for a new dock on 10 Nov. 1676 [MCC 1:31].

[26] Capt. Sylvester Salisbury, late commander at Albany, in his will, made on 26 Aug. 1679 and proved by 1680, named his wife Elizabeth executrix, with Jacob Tuni- son Kay and his brother-in-law, Peter Jacobs Marius, as overseers [Wills 1:66].

[27] Allard Anthony was sheriff of NYC in 1671 [Wills 1:66].

[28] Derrick Janson, ferryman, was commissioned ensign of foot on 27 Dec. 1689 [Eng. Mss. 34:142].

[29] Capt. Mathias Nicolls served as mayor of NYC. Letters of administration on his estate were granted his widow Abigail on 22 July 1693 [Wills 1:219-220].

[30] Grietye's son was apprenticed for 2 years to Arien Van Laer to learn the trade of shoemaker [RNA 5:243].

[31] Letters of administration were granted to Audry,

widow of Thomas Wandall, of Mespath Kills, L.I., on 20 May 1691 [Wills 1:183].

[32] In 1692 Augustin Herman had an attachment on the corn, horses and wagon of Hugo Barentson [RNA 6:386].

[33] John Lawrence, aged above 80, made his will on 7 Jan. 1698. It was proved on 15 May 1699 [Wills 1:307-308].

[34] Capt. John Manning was sheriff of NYC in 1667 [Eng. Mss. 22:17].

[35] Robert Hollis/Holles/Hallis was in court in 1673 and 1674 [RNA 7:5, 12, 48, 130].

[36] Thomas Hatfield was charged with bastardy in 1675 [Eng. Mss. 25:16].

[37] Hendrick Van Dyke, a surgeon, was made a burgher of New Amsterdam on 17 Apr. 1657 [Burchers 19 and Eng. Mss. 39:76].

[38] During the Dutch occupation some of the goods of Christopher Hoghland were seized in Boston [Eng. Mss. 25:71, 117].

[39] Richard Elliot, a guager under Lucas Santen [Eng. Mss. 35:28], on 12 Mar. 1676 married (2nd) Mrs. Catharine Cregier [Wills 1:142, 143].

[40] Alexander Bryan is described as of Connecticut [Eng. Mss. 25:245].

[41] Elizabeth Bedloo was the widow of Isaac Bedloo, merchant, who died intestate in Feb. 1672/3 [Wills 1:30].

[42] Walter Webly was summoned to prove that goods he brought from Barbados belonged to him [RNA 6:399]. He acted as agent of Lewis Morris and was trustee of the estate of Richard Morris [Eng. Mss. 24:2, 86].

[43] Letters of administration on the estate of George Cooke, gentleman, were granted to his widow Martha on 15 Feb. 1677 [Wills 1:47].

[44] Peter Jacobs, of Jamaica, L.I., was made freeman of NYC in 1698 as a bricklayer [Burghers 71].

[45] In 1684 William White, of Jamaica, L.I., petitioned to be allowed to keep a tavern there [Eng. Mss. 31:167].

[46] Thomas Taylor swore allegiance to the Crown on 24 Nov. 1675 [MCC 1:12].

[47] In 1677 Claus Burdinghe was taxed 8s. for his property at the water side [MCC 1:52].

[48] Anthony Waters, of Jamaica, L.I., in 1668 was appointed administrator of the estate of Thomas Stevenson [Wills 1:8]. On 23 May 1669 Anthony Waters, "clerk," wrote the will of Elizabeth Partridge, of Flushing [Wills 1:10]. His widow, Rachel, was appointed administratrix of his estate on 15 Apr. 1675 [Wills 1:29]

[49] In a suit in 1677 Samuel Blagge is described as of Stratford in New England [Eng. Mss. 26:63].

[50] William Merritt in 1695 was mayor of NYC [Burghers 58]

[51] Matthias De Haert was the natural son of Balthazar De Haert [Wills 1:59].

[52] Hendrick Willemsen Bakker in 1654 was condemned to pay fl. 800, the balance of the purchase of a

house [RNA 1:257].

[53] Daniel De Haert, chirurgeon, member of the Common Council in 1684, died late in 1689 or early in 1690 [Kenneth Scott, "New York Doctors and London Medicines, 1677," *Medical History* 11 (1967), p. 389, note 1].

[54] Martin Cregier was commissioned captain in 1670 [Eng. Mss. 22:106].

[55] John Henry was made a freeman of NYC on 7 Dec. 1675 [Burghers 40].

[56] John Smedes was a carter [RNA 6:360].

[57] Thomas Lovelace was sheriff of Richmond Co. in 1685 [Eng. Mss. 33:129].

[58] Samuel Rescoe, of Jamaica, L.I., apparently was an innkeeper in 1685 [Eng. Mss. 32:50]. He was an ensign in 1673 [Eng. Mss. 24:47].

[59] Audry, widow of John Sharpe, was appointed administratrix of his estate on 4 Feb. 1684 [Wills 1:166].

[60] Engeltie Peterse was the wife of Otto Gerritson, a tavern keeper [Wills 1:281].

[61] Col. Gabriel Minveille, merchant, mayor of NYC in 1684, married Susannah, daughter of John Lawrence. The colonel's will was proved on 1 Oct. 1702 [Wills 1:339-341].

[62] A liquor license was granted to a John Hendry on 23 Mar. 1680 [MCC 1:81].

[63] Fredrick Phillipse was the wealthiest man in NYC in his day. His will, made 26 Oct. 1700, was proved 9 Dec. 1702 [Wills 1:369-373].

[64] Jaques Coussou was made a freeman of New Amsterdam on 18 July 1658 [Burghers 25].

[65] On 12 Oct. 1675 John Manning prayed redress against Martine Hoffman, who mortgaged a house and lot in NYC after he had sold them to Manning [Eng. Mss. 24:185].

[66] Fredrick the cooper was probably Freryck Hendrick, cooper, who was dwelling in High St. in 1665 [RNA 5:222].

[67] Olof Stevense van Cortlandt was one of the three men commissioned in 1673 to settle the estate of the late Governor Lovelace [Eng. Mss. 23:142].

[68] Thomas Gibbs was sheriff of New York in 1675 [Eng. Mss. 24:173].

[69] Sigismundus Carman was probably the "Sigmomus" Lucas [MCC 1:34], a carman, otherwise referred to as Simonus Lucas, carman [MCC 1:73].

[70] Paulus Vander Beake was the son of Conradus Vander Beake, a measurer, by his first wife [Wills 1:435].

[71] Arent Isackson was dwelling in High St. in 1665 [RNA 5:222]. His wife was Styntie Laurens [*Baptisms from 1639 to 1730 in the Reformed Dutch Church, New York* (New York: The New York Genealogical and Biographical Society, 1901), p. 107].

[72] In 1673 Else Manning charged that Dr. Henry Taylor had assaulted her [RNA 7:8-9].

[73] In July 1671 Josiah Hunt and his wife Rebecca sued

Catherina, or Katherina, Harrison to recover goods
[RNA 6:302, 306].

[74]Claas Lock was a skipper [RNA 7:70].

[75]Nicholas Bayard was secretary to the Mayor's Court in
1671 [Wills 1:467] and Mayor of New York in 1686
[Wills 1:135].

[76]The Pardon in question was probably William Pardon,
who in 1680 was of Elizabethtown, N.J.
[Eng. Mss. 29:216, 217].

[77]Capt. Phillip Carteret was Governor of New Jersey in
1674 [Eng. Mss. 23:156].

[78]On 25 Mar. 1677 the Duke's farm in NYC was leased to
Dirck Seekers [Eng. Mss. 26:43].

[79]Jaculyne Turneur was perhaps the wife of Daniel Turneur, a deputy sheriff and overseer of Harlem
[RNA 5:326 and 6:282].

[80]Elizabeth or Lysbeth Nachtegaels was the wife of Mar-
cus de Soison [*Baptisms from 1639 to 1730 in the Reformed
Dutch Church, New York*, p. 96].

[81]On 6 Nov. 1712 Nathaniel Britton, James Garrison,
John Dove and John Bellue, of Richmond Co., petition-
ed for a license to keep a ferry on Staten Island
[Eng. Mss. 58:53].

[82]William Osburne, of Gravesend, L.I., in his will,
made 10 Feb. 1682 and proved 29 Aug. 1683, mentioned
his wife Alice, formerly the wife of Samuel Holmes
[Wills 1:469-470].

[83]Francis Doughty was a resident of Flushing, L.I.
[Wills 1:443].

[84]Audry, widow of John Sharpe, was made administratrix
of his estate on 4 Feb. 1684 [Wills 1:166[.

[85]In April 1685 Jane, widow of John Rider, petitioned
for letters of administration upon her late husband's
estate. [Eng. Mss. 31:106].

[86]In 1667 there was a disagreement between William
Shackerly, master of a ketch from New York, and Wil-
liam Critchlow, of St. Michaels, over damaged goods
[Eng. Mss. 26:140].

[87]Arent Jansen Moesman on 9 June 1668 by his attorney
demanded fl. 75 "hollands" from Allard Anthony
[RNA 7:131].

[88]Edward Dyre was a juror in a trial at a special court
held at New York on 13 July 1672 [RNA 6:382]. He
witnessed a codicil to the will of Capt. Thomas Delavall on 10 July 1692 [Wills 1:117].

[89]Samuel Edsal was made a burgher of New Amsterdam as a
hatter on 17 Apr. 1657 [RNA 7:153].

[90]Joseph Knott appeared in court on 21 Aug. 1671 as
agent for Benjamin Say [RNA 6:320].

[91]John Shackerly, merchant, in his will made 23 July
1679, mentioned his wife Sarah and his minor children
Elizabeth and William [Wills 1:63].

[92]The will of Thomas Lewis, merchant, was proved 14
June 1704 [Wills 1:389].

[93]Luycas Van Tienhoven, son of Cornelius Van Tienhoven
[Wills 1:221], was a surgeon [Eng. Mss. 38:131] and
owner of real estate in Pine St. in NYC [Wills 1:230].

[94]Capt. William Dyre was Mayor of NYC in 1680
[Wills 1:166].

[95]Egidius Luyck in 1674 was commissioned to value lots
along the North River [Eng. Mss. 23:409]. He prayed
to take the oath of allegiance in 1675 [Eng. Mss.
25:9-13].

[96]See note 66.

[97]Martha, widow of Cornellis Corsen of Staten Island,
yeoman, was confirmed on 7 Dec. 1692 as executrix of
her late husband's estate [Wills 1:230].

[98]Arien Cornelis was commissioned ensign on 10 Sept.
1684 [Eng. Mss. 33:43].

[99]George Downing, inhabitant of Oyster Bay, is on the
rate list on 29 Sept. 1683 [Lists of Inhabitants of
Colonial New York (Baltimore: Genealogical Publishing
Co., Inc., 1979), p. 148].

[100]Albert Bosch, cutler, was appointed inspector of
weights on 11 June 1672 [RNA 6:374]. His wife was
Elsie, daughter of Jurich and Catharine Blanck
[Wills 1:290].

[101]Cornelius Post was an innkeeper [Eng. Mss. 59:69].

[102]Richard Lockwood in 1675 sued John Cavalier for passage money from Virginia to Boston for Cavalier and
his wife [Eng. Mss. 24:55].

[103]John Cavalier, age 45, is 1690 deposed concerning the
will of Daniel De Hart [Wills 1:165].

[104]Joseph Hedger and his wife Hannah appear on a list of
inhabitants of Flushing in 1698 [Lists of Inhabitants of
Colonial New York (Baltimore: Genealogical Publishing
Co., Inc., 1979, p. 41].

[105]Peter Smith, of Jamaica, L.I. [Eng. Mss. 25:248] was
an undersheriff in June 1672 [Eng. Mss. 23:147].

[106]Margery Merritt, wife of William Merritt, who was commissioned lieutenant of a troop of horse on 21 Apr.
1686 [Eng. Mss. 33:235], collector of excise for NYC
in 1687 [Eng. Mss. 35:104] and one of the managers of
the building of Trinity Church in 1696 [Eng. Mss.
40:182]. His widow, Margery, on 20 Jan. 1709 petitioned for letters of administration on the estate of
Capt. John Tuder [Eng. Mss. 53:22].

[107]Anna, or Annetje, Claas Cressens (or Croezens) was the
widow of Daniel Litscho, who was deceased by 18 Apr.
1662 [RNA 4:64].

[108]In Feb. 1658 Beletje Jacobs sold a lot to Frerick
de Drayer [RNA 2:32].

[109]On 3 Oct. 1673 Tunis Craey was made measurer of apples,
onions and turnips [RNA 7:7].

[110]William Sturt in 1692 was town clerk of Pemaquid
[Eng. Mss. 38:200].

[111]Wessell Wessells was the eldest son of Peter Wessells
[Wills 1:350].

[112]Thomas De Lavall was captain and a member of Council [Wills 1:350].

[113]Martin Janse Meyer was granted by Gov. Colve the confiscated lot and house of Thomas De Lavall [Eng. Mss. 33:34-433].

[114]John Archer served as sheriff of NYC [Eng. Mss. 28:88].

[115]In 1675 Jacob Kipp opposed taking the oath of allegiance to the King [Eng. Mss. 24:186].

[116]David De Mareet was schepen and overseer of Harlem [RNA 6:36, 92].

[117]The will of Cornelis Jansen was proved on 18 Mar. 1705/6 [Wills 1:418-419].

[118]Jost Van Oblinus was overseer and schepen of Harlem [RNA 6:21, 88, 400].

[119]John or Johannes Dyckman was a baker [Wills 1:73].

[120]Bans of matrimony were published on 29 Apr. 1671 for Adolph Meyer, bachelor, born at Ulsen in Westphalia, with Maria Verveelen, born at Amsterdam [RNA 6:335].

[121]Nicholas De Meyer served as a schepen of New Amsterdam [RNA 5:16].

[122]The will of Thomas Coker, made on 8 May 1693, was witnessed by William Welch and Thomas Coker [Wills 1:248].

[124]See note 90. Knott served on a trial jury on 19 June 1671 [RNA 6:306]. On 15 Nov. 1676 he was in prison for having shipped unculled staves contrary to law, was tried and convicted [Eng. Mss. 25:249-252].

[125]Cornelis Van Borsum was overseer of the estate of Joost Adrians [Wills 1:69].

[126]Abell Hardenbrooke was a shoemaker. His wife was Annetie [Eng. Mss. 28:148].

[127]See note 46.

[128]Anna Elizabeth Wessells, widow of Warner Wessells, on 6 Aug. 1675 was granted a license to marry Francis Rumbouts [Eng. Mss. 24:127].

[129]Rem Jansen, a smith [RNA 4:344], on 3 Nov. 1664 sold a house to Walter Salter [RNA 6:5].

[130]Roelof Jansen was a mason [Burghers 22].

[131]Gerrardus Wessell is mentioned in the will of his sister, Christian Teller, widow of Jacob Teller [Wills 1:301].

[132]John Garland, or Gerland, in his will made 15 July 1673, named as executors his brother, Gulian Ver Planck, and his friend, Francis Rumbouts [Wills 1:28].

[133]Francis Rumbouts, merchant, served as an alderman [Wills 1:188-189].

[134]Gelyne Verplanck in 1674 was fined for corresponding with the New Englanders [Eng. Mss. 23:232, 233].

[135]James Mathews, an innkeeper, named his wife Mary as executrix in his will that was proved on 16 Mar. 1685 [Wills 1:134].

[136]Jan Spiegelaer was a tavern-keeper [RNA 7:6].

[137]Isaac Van Vleck was a brewer. His will was proved in 1688 [Wills 1:252-253].

[138]The wife of Jan Speiglaer may have been Gerritie.

[139]See note 92. Geesie, widow of Thomas Lewis, was appointed executrix of his estate in 1684 [Eng. Mss. 31:170].

[140]Nielis Matysen was overseer of Harlem in 1666 [RNA 6:15].

[141]In Feb. 1674 Gerrit Hendrickse, butcher, obtained from Gov. Colve a patent to a house and lot, formerly the property of William Pattison, "now residing in Scotland" [Eng. Mss. 38:433].

[142]On the night between the 16th and 17th of Jan. 1674 Jacob Smith, a turner, made trouble at the house of Francis Leigh and was brought to the City Hall by the watch [RNA 7:48].

[143]The open boat of Cornelis the fisher was in dockage arrears on 23 Feb. 1683/4 [MCC 1:28].

[144]Johanes Van Cowenhoven, secretary, whose wife was named Sara, made his will in June 1690, and it was proved in Nov. of that year [Wills 1:163-164].

[145]On 15 Feb. 1695/6 a marriage license was granted to Christopher Hoaglandt and Sarah Willett [Wills 1:262].

[146]Richard Elliott, cooper, on 13 May 1693 made his will, which was proved 3 July 1694. He mentioned his wife Susannah and sons Robert, Joseph, Henry and John [Wills 1:237-238].

[147]On Joseph Lee see also MCC 1:123.

[148]Lowrens Vander Spiegel served as a city constable and schepen [RNA 6:265, 397].

[149]Reinier Willemsen was a baker [RNA 1:104].

[150]Probably Timotheus de Gabry, secretary and schepen of New Amsterdam [RNA 5:17 and 7:168]. He was deceased by June 1680 [Eng. Mss. 29:125].

[151]Mrs. Hawkins was Sarah Hawkins, who on 30 Mar. 1671 was appointed administratrix of the estate of her late husband, John Hawkins, late a resident of Elk River, Maryland [Wills 1:15-16].

[152]Mrs. Johns was doubtless Mary Johns, who on 15 Apr. 1675 was appointed administratrix of the estate of her husband Philip [Wills 1:29].

[153]Thomas Ashton served as sheriff of NYC [Eng. Mss. 25:221].

[154]Samuel Willson is described as "of London" [Eng. Mss. 22:76].

[155]Antonio De Milt was schout in 1674 [Eng. Mss. 23:332]; in 1675 he refused to take the oath of allegiance under Gov. Andros [Eng. Mss. 24:186].

[156]Elias Doughtey, of Flushing, L.I., was a coronet in 1673 [Eng. Mss. 24:50, 51]. He was commissioned a justice of the peace in Oct. 1685 [Eng. Mss. 33:193].

[157]Dirck Smith in 1663 brought Foppe Outhout from the South River to New Amsterdam [RNA 5:333].

[158]Adrian Van der Donck was sheriff of Renselaerswyck
in 1642 [Dutch Mss. 4:148].

[159]John Rider on 11 May 1684 was appointed clerk and
register of Westchester Co. [Eng. Mss. 33:4]. His
widow Jane in Apr. 1685 petitioned to be appointed
administratrix of his estate [Eng. Mss. 31:106].

[160]Isaac Melyn on 16 June 1684 gave a deed for a house
and lot in the Prince's Graft to Isaac Van Vleck
[Eng. Mss. 33:71]. Van Vleck was commissioned lieutenant on 10 Sept. 1684 [Eng. Mss. 33:43]. On 3
Nov. 1684 Alderman Van Vleck was commissioned a
justice of the peace [Eng. Mss. 33:65]. An "Ancor
annys" was an anker of anisette.

[161]John Williams was defendant in July 1674 in a case
between him and Capt. Thomas Freesell [RNA 7:108].

[162]Hartmann Wessells on 31 Oct. 1673 demanded fl. 40
for curing the maid of Henry Taylor and for her
board and drink [RNA 7:17].

[163]Jacob Lendertsen was overseer of roads in June 1671
[RNA 6:375] and schepen of New Harlem in Aug. 1673
[RNA 6:401]. In 1670 he and his wife, Rebecca
Frerericksen, petitioned for redress of injustice
done her by her late father's will [Eng. Mss. 29:4].
He was granted a liquor license on 24 Apr. 1680
[MCC 1:81].

[164]On 27 Sept. 1674 Jan Theunissen and others petitioned for a grant of land on Staten Island [Eng. Mss.
23:399]. Jan Tunison and others on 5 Oct. 1691 were
seen to roll out of the goose house of Mr. Townley
barrels of pork and beef and sell the same for drink
[Eng. Mss. 38:36-40].

[165]Dirrick Evertz was a city creditor in 1676/7
[MCC 1:45].

[166]Jacobus Vande Water, of Brooklyn, was a notary public
[Wills 1:231].

[167]Susanna Garland was the wife of John Garland, whose
will was recorded on 26 Feb. 1674 [Wills 1:28].

[168]Mary Johns, widow, on 15 Apr. 1675 was appointed administratrix of the estate of her deceased husband
Philip [Wills 1:29].

[169]Cornelis Steenwyck was a member of Council in 1672
[Wills 1:25].

[170]Paulus Richards was a prominent merchant [Wills 1:40]

[171]William Welch was doorkeeper and messenger of the
House of Representatives in 1692 [Eng. Mss. 38, 102].

[172]The property of Francis Lee was taxed on 24 July 167'
[MCC 1:54].

[173]George Davis was made a freeman of NYC on 27 May
1702 as a cordwainer [Burghers 78].

[174]Assur Levy owned a slaughter house and pen without
the water gate [Wills 1:123]. Letters of administration on his estate were granted his widow Maria
on 24 Apr. 1682 [Wills 1:112].

[175]Robert Hollis/Holles was sued for debt on 28 Sept.
1673 by Jan Hendrick van Gunst [RNA 5:12, 48].
See note 35.
[176]William Bogardus was appointed treasurer of NYC on
24 Feb. 1679/80 [MCC 1:75].
[177]On 18 Sept. 1674 John Chatlin and John Ward charged
that Emanuel Mandevell took from them without their
consent a canoe which never re-appeared
[RNA 7:120].
[178]John Shackerly on 10 Nov. 1676 was taxed for a new
dock [MCC 1:32]. In April 1693 his widow, Sarah
Burger, petitioned concerning ground leading to the
fortification called the Oyster Pasty [MCC 1:321].
[179]On 24 Jan. 1676 Josias Hillman was granted a writ of
appeal in a suit between him and John Tudor [Eng.
Mss. 25:69].
[180]William Sturt was town clerk of Pemaquid [Eng. Mss.
38:200].
[181]On 8 May 1663 Styntje Lauwerens was in default in a
suit against her by Merritje Jacobs [RNA 4:238]. In
1663 John Denman had promised to pay money to
Styntje [RNA 4:262]. In 1670 Johannes Witthart was
suing Styntje [RNA 6:271].
[182]Sgt. Ashton was doubtless the Thomas Ashton who on
14 Oct. 1678 was appointed sheriff [MCC 1:69].
[183]In March 1670 Capt. Dudley Lovelace was one of the
commissioners for the affairs of Esopus and the new
villages adjacent [Eng. Mss. 22:99].
[184]George Cooke's property was taxed for a new dock in
Nov. 1676 [MCC 1:44]. On 1 Mar. 1674 he petitioned
for leave to go to Rhode Island [Eng. Mss. 23:316].
On 26 July 1677 Hezekiah Usher in Boston sent a
power of attorney to George Cooke, of New York, to
prosecute Ezekiel Fogg [Eng. Mss. 26:76]. Letters of
administration on Cooke's estate were granted on 15
Feb. 1677 to Mrs. Martha Cooke [Wills 1:47].
[185]Henry Nuton [Newton] on 9 July 1667, by order of the
governor, was chosen marshal of court of Burgomasters
and Schepens [RNA 6:84-85]. He was also mace-bearer
[RNA 6:260].
[186]Samuel Edsall, a hatter, obtained the small burgher
right [RNA 7:153].
[187]Adolph Pietersen, a carpenter [MCC 1:196], was elected assessor of the Dock Ward in 1691 [MCC 1:214]. He
was "lately deceased" on 20 Nov. 1694 [MCC 1:272].
[188]Gerrit Huygen de Kleyn was a surgeon [RNA 7:11]. He
married Geertie Rutgers, widow of Harmen Wessels
[RNA 6:262].
[189]Leendert [or Leonard] Huygen De Kleyn was made freeman of NYC on 30 Aug. 1698 as a baker [Burghers 67].
The location of his house in 1709 near the East River
is described [MCC 2:374-375].
[190]On complaint of Thomas Cornish and his guardian, Caleb
Levereth, it is ordered that Cornish be released from

his apprenticeship to Dr. Thomas Taylor
[RNA 7:16, 29, 31].

[191]On 29 Nov. 1673 Gov. Colve granted the patent of a
plantation formerly belonging to Major Nathaniel
Kingsland, of Barbados [Eng. Mss. 23:1-433].

[192]Samuel Leete, an attorney, was aged 39 on 11 Feb.
1677 [Wills 1:47]. He served as an alderman and as
clerk of the Court of Mayor and Aldermen [Wills 1:65].

[193]Jan Jansen Verein [or Veryn] on 17 June had mortgaged
all his property to Schepen Timotheus Gabry
[RNA 4:21].

[194]Timotheus Gabriell (Timotheus Gabry/Gabrie) served
as schepen, city collector and inspector of bread
[RNA 5:185, 254 and 6:266].

[195]Domine Jacobus Fabricius swore allegiance to the
Crown on 24 Nov. 1675 [MCC 1:12]. He was a Lutheran
clergyman and was refused permission to baptize
[Eng. Mss. 23:237].

[196]On 29 Nov. 1673 Gov. Colve granted a patent of land
at Achter Coll to Abraham Pierson, Sr., and others
[Eng. Mss. 23:1-433].

[197]John Arnold on 16 Dec. 1680 wrote to Gov. Andros
soliciting the position of clerk of the sessions for
the East Riding of Long Island [Eng. Mss. 30:266].

[198]Magdeline Cowenhoven was probably the Widow Cowenhoven mentioned in Oct. 1674 in connection with a
lot of Elizabeth Drisius that adjoined Magdeline's
property [Eng. Mss. 24:57-433].

[199]The house of the widow of John Evertson Karsboome is
mentioned in Jan. 1686/7 [MCC 1:185].

[200]Joseph Yates served in one of the independent companies in New York [Eng. Mss. 59:105].

[201]In 1696 a certain Force, possibly Matthew, in
Jamaica, L.I., was to be arrested as a deserter
[Eng. Mss. 40:196].

[202]Anthony Brockholls was Governor of New York in 1678
[Eng. Mss. 27:4].

[203]Samuel Lane, late a soldier in the garrison in NYC,
was deceased by 26 Apr. 1675, when a fellow soldier,
one Wardroppe, was appointed administrator of Lane's
estate [Wills 1:29].

[204]Styntie Lourens was sued for debt in 1663 by
Merritje Jacobs [RNA 4:238, 262] and in 1670 by
Johannes Witthart [RNA 6:271].

[205]Sharpe's wife was named Audry [Wills 1:166].

[206]Walter Carr was taxed for a new dock on 10 Nov.
1676 [MCC 1:36].

[207]A laced whiske was a neckerchief worn by women in
the latter half of the 17th century.

[208]The will of Robert Story, merchant, was proved on
15 June 1683, and his wife Patience was named executrix [Wills 1:243].

[209]William Allen was taxed in 1676 and 1677
[MCC 1:35, 52].

[210]On 14 Dec. 1686 an inventory of the estate of George Masters was presented; his wife Mary was confirmed as executrix [Wills 1:138].

[211]Henry Willis was a Quaker. He was in Flushing in 1680 and in Hempstead in 1687 [Eng. Mss. 29:202, 220 and 35:122].

[212]The proceedings in the case of Townsend vs. Foxhall are found in Eng. Mss. 24:108.

[213]Isaac Melyn shared in the recovery of silver from a wrecked Spanish ship near the Bahamas [Wills 1:87-88].

[214]Derrick the Wollspinner in Nov. 1676 was taxed for a new dock [MCC 1:36].

[215]Sarah Tenix was the wife of Isaac De Forrest [Wills 1:210].

[216]Thomas Vardon was listed as a city creditor in 1677, and his house in the Smiths Street Lane was taxed in that year [MCC 1:44 and 58].

[217]Erve is a variant of erf, "cattle."

[218]On 6 Apr. 1680 the wife of Josias Hallett was ordered banished from NYC [MCC 1:79]. In 1684 Josias was in dockage arrears for an open boat [MCC 1:129].

[219]Boelen Roeloffs was the father of Hendrick Boelen (a smith) [Wills 1:209].

[220]Alexander Bryan of Connecticut in 1676 obtained a warrant against Mrs. Elizabeth Bedloo to satisfy judgments against her [Eng. Mss. 25:246].

[221]Peter Paulusen in 1674 was charged with assaulting Jacob Wolphertsen and others [Eng. Mss. 23:392]. In 1667 Pieter Poulsen sued Warnaer Wessels for reparation of character [RNA 6:97-98]. In 1669 Poulsen was ordered to pay a debt of 30 guilders to Richard Cornwall [RNA 6:206].

[222]Michael Smith, probably the son of Jacob Smith (a turner) and Mary his wife [Wills 1:95], served on juries in 1671 [RNA 6:322, 343]. In 1676 he was taxed for a new dock and the next year for real estate [MCC 1:33, 52].

[223]Capt. James Bullain/Bolleyn/Bollain/Bollyn in 1665 sued Dirck Storm for an anker of brandy and it is recorded that he served on juries [RNA 5:267, 279, 284, 292, 298, 336, 337].

[224]Capt. Thomas Badgard/Badford/Badger in 1671 was appointed to examine a difference between Richard Ripley, master of the pink Batchelors Delight, and his seamen [RNA 6:342]. Badgord, described as a merchant, died intestate in 1672, and administrators on his estate were appointed on 15 Oct. 1672 [Wills 1:26].

[225]In 1680 Richard Hall sued William Darvall, and in December of the next year the King in council confirmed the judgment of the Court of Assizes in favor of Hall. A receipt was then signed on 7 Dec. by Hannah Hall, administratrix [Eng. Mss. 30:54]. On 2 Nov. 1681 Hannah was appointed administratrix of the

estate of her husband, described as "lately drowned" [Wills 1:110].

[226] William Rodney, Surveyor of Customs, when bound for the island of Nevis on board a vessel named *Lovell*, died on board in the Sound near New Haven. Letters of administration on his estate were granted in Jan. 1678 to Capt. John Fowler of Staten Island [Wills 1:56-57].

[227] Joseph Lee, formerly haven master of NYC [MCC 1:123], in 1684 was appointed clerk and register of Westchester Co. [Eng. Mss. 33:50].

[228] Peter Gerritsen in 1675 was charged with mutiny on board the *Susannah* of Jamaica, Andrew Ball master, off New Utrecht [Eng. Mss. 24:126].

[229] Henry Brasier, by his will dated 23 Apr. 1689, left his estate to his wife Susannah [Wills 1:245].

[230] John Carman, of Hempstead, L.I., testified on 12 July 1677 as to payment to Indians for their land [Eng. Mss. 26:71]. He probably married Hannah, daughter of John Seaman the elder, of Hempstead [Wills 1:249-250].

[231] Arian Laer was probably the Adrian Van Laer who obtained the burgher right on 18 July 1658 [Burghers 25]. He was a shoemaker [RNA 5:243].

[232] The property of Elias Provost in the Smiths Street was taxed in July 1677 [MCC 1:57]. In 1672 Elias Provoost, smith, was dwelling at the Heere Gracht [Wills 1:59].

[233] John Budd, of Southold, L.I., on 30 May 1684 was commissioned lieutenant of a troop of horse on Long Island [Eng. Mss. 33:10]. His will was proved on 12 Nov. 1684 [Wills 1:166].

[234] Andrew Ball was master of the *Susannah*, of Jamaica [Eng. Mss. 24:122-123, 125].

[235] Thomas Coker in 1685 was commissioned coroner [Eng. Mss. 33:110 and MCC 1:205] and as member of the common council for the West Ward [MCC 1:214]. He was commissioned Surveyor of the Custom House on 12 July 1686 [Eng. Mss. 33:266]. He witnessed the will of Robert Shaw in 1686 [Wills 1:137] and of Richard Tinker in 1693 [Wills 1:248].

[236] Henry Clarke, of Poynig Creek, Virginia, lately come from Virginia, made his will on 26 May 1679. It was proved 19 July [Wills 1:54].

[237] Capt. John Collier/Colier on 30 July 1675 witnessed the will of Roger Rugg [Wills 1:468]. He was appointed sheriff for the year 1680-81 [MCC 1:146].

[238] Cornelis Van Bursen/Borsum on 14 Oct. 1673 received the patent of a lot in Manhattan for the services of his wife Sara as Indian interpreter [Eng. Mss. 23:20-433]. In his will, made 16 June 1680 and proved 25 Sept. 1682, he named his wife Sarah executrix [Wills 1:120-121].

[239]On 2 Nov. 1674 a caveat was entered by John Saffin against Henry van de Water's selling a house in New York [Eng. Mss. 24:3]. Hendrick van de Water was a skipper [RNA 7:70].

[240]In 1676/7 John Van Bommell was listed as a city creditor [MCC 1:45]. In 1668 he appraised carpenter's tools at the request of Marretie Gerrits and Mary Goosens [RNA 6:156]. He died, blind, in 1693 [Wills 1:220-221].

[241]In 1680 Paulus Richards was suing Peter Peterson [Eng. Mss. 29:244-247]. Pieter Pieterzen was granted the burgher right as a carpenter on 17 Apr. 1657 [Burghers 23].

[242]Jacobus Vandewater was commissioned town major of New Orange on 1 Jan. 1674 [Eng. Mss. 23:188]. In 1687 he was a notary public in Kings Co. [Wills 1:231]. He was commissioned clerk of Kings Co. on 20 Dec. 1689 [Eng. Mss. 36:142].

[243]John Watkins was appointed carman on 5 May 1679 [MCC 173 and RNA 6:360].

[244]Paulus Richards, merchant [Wills 1:143], was elected alderman of the South Ward on 14 Oct. 1687 [MCC 1:191].

[245]Johannes Verveile was taxed for a new dock in Nov. 1676 and for real estate in July 1677 [MCC 1:33, 59]. In Feb. 1671/2 he was appointed constable and clerk of Fordham [RNA 6:362]. His wife was Anneke Jaartvelt [RNA 4:67]. He was elected constable of Harlem in 1666 [RNA 6:8], obtained the position of ferryman in Harlem and was chosen overseer there in 1667 [RNA 6:83, 92].

[246]The property of Peter Janson Van Werkendam in the High Street was taxed in July 1677 [MCC 1:56]. In 1659 he had produced evidence that he enclosed with a fence the land of Pieter Lefebure, where he resided, before he left it [RNA 3:44-45].

[247]Mr. Adolph was probably Peter Adolph, who served as assessor, assistant and brand master in the East Ward [MCC 1:191, 204, 212].

[248]William White was a hatter [RNA 7:125].

[249]Ephraim Heermans/Herman was city clerk and collector of wharf dues [RNA 6:364 and 7:29] and secretary of the city [RNA 7:122].

[250]In 1675 Robert Lapraire/Leprerie/Laprairee obtained a judgment against Jacob Melyne [Eng. Mss. 24:170]. On 14 May 1678 Laprairie wrote from Woodbridge to Capt. Brockholls asking that a runaway Frenchman be arrested [Eng. Mss. 27:99]. In April 1692 he petitioned for compensation for goods taken from him by soldiers [Eng. Mss. 38:92].

[251]Jacob Melyn was one of those who in 1683 participated in salvaging silver from a wrecked Spanish vessel near the Bahama Islands [Wills 1:87-88].

[252] Helike, the widow of Cornelius Clopper (a black-smith), married Shuart Olpherts [Wills 1:99].

[253] William Pattison, living in Scotland, was claiming his real estate in High Street that had been confiscated by Gov. Cole and sold to Nicholas Bayard [Eng. Mss. 23:16-433].

[254] Lodewyck Post, or Pos, in 1658 was captain of the Rattle Watch of New Amsterdam [RNA 7:198] and in 1672 was Provost Marshal of NYC [RNA 6:371].

[255] Derrick Eversen Floyd, boatman, was taxed on his property in NYC in 1677 [MCC 1:50]. When he was sued in 1674 by Catharine Lane, the court ordered that Stephanus Van Cortland and Johannes Vermillje reconcile the parties [RNA 7:78, 81].

[256] Pieter Harmensen was a ship-carpenter [RNA 5:273].

[257] Cornelis Van Ruyven, son-in-law of Domine Megapolensis, served as secretary, alderman, church warden, receiver of the West India Co. and burgomaster [RNA 1:211; 2:46; 5:167; 6:103, 201, 396].

[258] Philip Udale was taxed in the town of Huntington, L.I., in 1675 [Lists of Inhabitants of Colonial New York (Baltimore: Genealogical Publishing Co., 1979), p.65].

[259] John Jos. Ludly was taxed in the town of Jamaica, L.I., in 1683 [Lists of Inhabitants of Colonial New York, p. 141].

[260] Letters of administration on the estate of Ralph Hutchinson, of Newcastle, Delaware, were granted on 20 June 1682 to William Darvall and James Matthews [Wills 1:114].

[261] Katherine Purchase in Nov. 1676 was taxed for a new dock [MCC 1:35] and on 1 July 1680 was granted a liquor license [MCC 1:81].

[262] As in 1670 Henry Hedger was ordered by the court to pay Ambrosius De Weerhem for three carpenter's plaines or to give them back, Hedger may have been a carpenter [RNA 6:225].

[263] Margaret Stevenson was the wife of Isaac Stevenson, mariner [Wills 1:283].

[264] Mary, wife of Gerritt Van Tright, on 22 Aug. 1701 deposed relative to the birth of Abraham Governeur in Amsterdam, Holland [Eng. Mss. 44:157]. In 1661 and 1664 Gerritt was nominated for schepen [RNA 3:260 and 5:17] and in 1669 for alderman [RNA 6:201].

[265] John Robinson was appointed alderman of the West Ward in 1683 [MCC 1:113]. He also served as a justice of the peace [Eng. Mss. 33:65].

[266] Suart Olpherts in 1676 was supervisor of buildings and pavements [MCC 1:21]. He served as assessor, constable and assistant of the West Ward. His will was proved on 5 Oct. 1702 [Wills 1:343].

[267] Frederick Hoy was probably Frederick Hay, a cooper

[MCC 1:55].

[268]Cornelis Wynhart/Wynhaert/Winehart, "of Dellowar," was admitted a burgher on 11 June 1672 [RNA 6:374]. He was granted a liquor license on 1 Oct. 1680 [MCC 1:81].

INDEX

Hall, George 33; Hannah 73; Richard 48, 49, 73
Hallett/Hallet, Josiah/Josias 44, 73
Hambleton, Robert 59
Hans, - Mr. 40
Hardenbrooke, Abell 16, 26, 33, 38, 49, 54, 58, 68;
     Annetie 68
Harmanson/Harmensen, Ephraim 55; Pieter/Peter 56, 76
Harrison, - Widow 40; Joseph 38; Katherina/Catharina/
     Katherne/Kath. 8, 12, 17, 24, 31, 66
Hatfield/Hatfeld, Thomas/Tho. 3, 26, 32, 64
Hawkins, - Mrs. 25; John 69; Sarah 69
Hayes, Sarah 44
Haymor, Richd. 1
Hedger/Hodger, Hannah 67; Henry/Hen. 57, 62, 76; Joseph
     13, 17, 67
Hellman, Hannah 33; Josia 33
Hendricks/Hendrick/Hendrickse/Hendrix/Hendrixon,
     Freryck (see Fredrick the cooper); Geesie 63;
     Gerrit 20, 27, 69
Hendry/Henry, John 5, 6, 8, 21, 65
Herman/Heermans, Augustin 64; Ephraim 75
Hiatt, Walter 1
Hillman, Josias 71
Hoffman, Martine 7, 65
Hoghland, - Mr. 40; Christopher 4, 23, 64, 69
Hollis/Holles/Hallis, Robert 3, 26, 32, 64, 71
Holmes, Alice 66; Samuel 66
Hoy/Hay, Frederick 60, 76
Hugo, Gerrit 34, 39, 41
Hunt, Josiah 65; Rebecca 65
Hutchinson, Ralph 56, 76

Isackson/Isaxon, Arent/Arian/Arient 8, 13, 14, 18, 28,
     38, 43, 65

Jacobs, Barnard 1; Beletje 67; Merritje 71, 72; Peter/
     Pet./P., 5, 11, 15, 24, 32, 58, 64
Janson/Jansen, Cornelis 14, 68; Derrick 2, 63; John 49;
     Mary 63; Rem 68; Roelof/Roloph 18, 68
Jenkins, Anto. 31
Jeremias, - Mr. 54
Johns, - Mrs. 25, 29; Mary 69, 70; Philip 69, 70
Jonson/Johnson, Josias/Josia/Josi. 24, 31, 48; Ram 27,
     31, 32
Josten, John 15
Jourdaine, John 51

Karsboome, John Evertson 40, 72
Kay, Jacob Tunison 63
Kingsland, - Major 37; Nathaniel 72
Kipp, Jacob 14, 20, 29, 68
Knott, Joseph/Josep./Jos. 11, 15, 66, 68
Kyckout, Jon. 1

Laer/VanLaer, Arian/Adrian 49, 52, 59, 63, 74
Lane/Laine, Catharine 76; Samuell 40, 72
Langestraat/Longstraet, Jan./Jon. 1. 62
Lawrence/Laurens/Lauwerens/Lourens, - Mr. 31, 36, 37;
        John 1, 3, 4, 6, 10, 16, 19, 23, 29, 38, 41, 42,
        43, 44, 64, 65; Jos. 40; Styntje/Styntie/
        Steentye/Steentie 34, 41, 65, 71, 72; Susannah
        65
Lee/Leigh, - Mr. 23, 58; Francis 1, 20, 31, 69, 70;
        Joseph/Jos. 24, 48, 69, 74
Leeds, William 42
Leete, - Mr. 38, Samuel 72
Lefebure, Pieter 75
Lenderson/Lendertsen/Leenderson, Jacob 28, 33, 70
Leprerye/Leprery/Leprerie/Laprairee/Lapraire, Robert 55,
        59, 75
Levereth, Caleb 71
Levy, Assur 32, 70; Maria 70
Lewis, Geesie 69; Thomas 11, 20, 24, 26, 32, 35, 50,
        66, 69
Litscho/Litscoe, Anna/Annatje 13, 17, 67; Daniel 67
Lock, Claas/Claus 9, 12, 17, 25, 66
Lockerman, - Mr. 40; Govert 63; Jacob 2, 63
Lockwood, Richard 12, 67
Lovelace/Lovlace, - Col. 9, 35; - Gov. 65; Dudley 35,
        71; Francis/Fran. 9, 34, 37; Thomas/Tho. 5, 7,
        10, 12, 16, 23, 31, 36, 41, 59, 65
Lucas, Sigmomus/Simonus/Sym. 1, 8, 62, 65
Ludly/Luidley, John Jos./John 56, 76
Luyck/Luyke/Luke, Egidius/Egidias 11, 29, 37, 47, 56, 67

Mandevile, Emanuel/Emanuell 33, 37, 43, 50, 71
Manera, Nicolas 53, 55
Manning, - Capt. 32; Alice/Else 8, 12, 17, 24, 31, 65;
        John, 3, 4, 5, 7, 11, 12, 13, 17, 25, 32, 36,
        64, 65
Marius, Peter Jacobs 63
Masters, George 42, 73; Mary 73
Matthews/Mathewes, James/Jam. 19, 26, 31, 53, 54, 68,
        76; Mary 68
Matysen/Matyson/Mattyson/Mathiason, Nelis/Nielis 20, 26,
        32, 69
Meade, Peter Janson 21
Megapolensis, - Domine 76
Melyn, Isaac 70, 73; Jacob 75
Merritt/Merrit, Margery 13, 67; William/Wm. 5, 64, 67
Meyer/Mayor, Adolph 14, 68; Maria 68; Martine/Martin
        Janse 14, 18, 58, 60, 68
Minas, John 1
Minviele/Minveille, - Mr. 15, 31, 36, 37, 40, 47, 48,
        49; Gabriel/Gabriell/Gabr./Gab. 1, 3, 4, 6, 9,
        10, 12, 17, 22, 25, 29, 42, 49, 52, 54, 59, 65;
        Susannah 65
Moesman, Arent Jansen 66

Van Brughen, Joannes 29
Van Bursen/Van Borsum, Cornelis/Corn./Co. 11, 15, 24,
      52, 54, 56, 68, 74; Sarah 74
Van Cleyfe/Van Cleyffe/Van Cleafe/Van Cleife/Van Cleaf,
      - Mr. 40; Dirick/Dirrick 2, 5, 7, 9, 11, 31, 58,
      63
Van Cortlandt/Van Cortland/Van Courtland, Olave
      Stephens/Olof Stevense 25, 65; Stephanus/Stephen
      44, 47, 76
Van Cowenhoven, Johanes 69; Sara 69
Van Der Beek/Vander Beake, Conradus 65; Paulus 8, 12,
      62, 65
Van Der Donck, Adrian 70
Vander Spiegle/Vander Spiegel/Vanderspeigle, Lawrence/
      Lowrens/Lowr. 24, 25, 31, 46, 69
Van De Water/Vandewater/Vande Water/Vande Watter,
      Hendrick/Henry 52, 54, 75; Jacob/Jacobus/Jac.
      28, 53, 55, 56, 57, 70, 75
Van Dyke/Vandyke, Hendrick/Henry 3, 7, 11, 26, 34, 36,
      64
Van Gunst, Jan Hendrick 71
Van Oblinus, Jost 14, 68
Van Ruyven/VanRuyvens, Cornelius 56, 76
Van Tienhoven/Tienhoven/Tenenhoven, Cornelius 67;
      Luycas/Lucas/Luyc. 11, 24, 37, 41, 46, 67
Van Tricht/Van Tright, Gerritt 58, 76; Mary 76
Van Vleck, Isaac/Isack 20, 27, 69, 70
Van Werkendam, Peter Janson/P. Janson 54, 60, 75
Verdon/Vardon, Thomas 43, 73
Vermillje, Johannes 76
Verplanck, Gelyne/Gulian 18, 58, 68
Verveile/Verveelen, Anneke 75; Johannes/Joannes 53, 75;
      Maria 68

Walsgrave, George/Geo. 1, 62
Walton, Tho. 57
Wandall, Audry 63; Thomas/Tho. 2, 57, 64
Waram, Abram. 1
Ward, John 71
Wardroppe/Wardrupp, - 72; Allex. 40
Waters, Anthony 5, 64; Rachel 64
Watkins, John 1, 53, 62, 75
Webly/Webley, - Mr. 53; Walter 4, 5, 6, 10, 16, 24, 33,
      64
Weekes, John 43
Welch, William 1, 31, 62, 68, 70
Wessells/Wessell, Anna Elizabeth/Anna Eliz./Anna 18, 19
      26, 27, 31, 68; Bart. 60; Eliz. 32; Gerrardus 18
      68; Harmen 71; Hartmann 28, 51, 70; Peter 1, 62,
      67; Warner/Warnaer 68, 73; Wessell 13, 18, 28,
      38, 43, 67
West, - Mr. 48; John 2, 63
White, William 1, 5, 8, 44, 47, 55, 58, 59, 62, 64, 75
Willemsen, Reinier 69

NO SURNAME

www.ingramcontent.com/pod-product-compliance
Lightning Source LLC
Chambersburg PA
CBHW071139280326
41935CB00010B/1287